P9-CCX-080

# COOKING

## WITH

# CONFIDENCE

*Inspirations for Good Food at Home*

# COOKING

## WITH

# CONFIDENCE

*Inspirations for Good Food at Home*

*Eunice Naomi Wiebolt*

Tony Martin Photography

ROMARIN PUBLISHING CO.
Minnesota

Romarin Publishing Co.
1945 Red Oak Drive SW
Brainerd, MN 56401
romarin@scicable.com

Book design by Eunice Naomi Wiebolt
Photographs by Tony Martin
Nature Prints by Eunice Naomi Wiebolt
Project Coordinator - Kelly S. Dorholt
Technical Advisor - David D. Dorholt

Printed in the United States of America by Bang Printing

Library of Congress Cataloging-In-Publication Data:

Wiebolt, Eunice Naomi.
Cooking with confidence : inspirations for good food at home /
Eunice Naomi Wiebolt ; Tony Martin Photography.
p. cm.
Includes index.
LCCN 2002091141
ISBN 0-9718894-0-6

1. Cookery.   I. Title.
TX714.W515 2003    641.5
QBI03-200290

ISBN 0-9718894-0-6
10 9 8 7 6 5 4 3 2 1
First Edition

Cover: Flourless Chocolate Cake, page 162
Back Cover: Walleye Cakes, page 129
Shrimp Pasta Salad, page 133

# Dedication

COOKING WITH CONFIDENCE
is dedicated to my husband, Ken,
to our five sons and daughters-in-law,
and to our precious grandchildren

who have all given me their unwavering
love, encouragement, taste testing time,
and critiques throughout this project;

to my brothers and sisters, and
to the memory of Mom and Dad.

*Eunice Naomi Wiebolt*

# Acknowledgments

Sincere Thanks

to Rae Skinner
for being my food assistant during the photography sessions

to Karen Kreiser and Bridget Lindner
for their critical recipe testing

to Laurie Jacobi and Jay Witta
for their professional opinions

and to my family and many friends for their encouragement, support,
and tastings during this project.

Eunice Naomi Wiebolt

# Table of Contents

# Introduction
## COOKING WITH CONFIDENCE

This book has had a long beginning, having spent decades in the world of dreams and wishes. Since early childhood I have been passionate about good food and good cooking.

I am the 10th child of 13 born into a hardworking Minnesota farm family. Someone was always cooking or talking about cooking at our house. And with a family of that size, you can imagine it was never quiet. We were each expected to contribute to our self-sufficient life. If we were not working in the fields, we were expected to feed those who were. If we were not picking the apples, we were making apple pies - 10 at a time - for the freezer. Depending on the buddy system of each-one-help one, we learned as we practiced, and our experiments in the kitchen are legendary. We used what we had, and made it work. Simple menus and simple meals from the pantry and garden were the normal, expected fare.

I remember the day my first Home Economics teacher had to prove to me that 3 teaspoons equaled 1 tablespoon. At our house, the teaspoon I used was a teaspoon from the table, and 2 of those always equaled the big spoon I had called a tablespoon, which was actually a serving spoon. It was my first experience at accurate measuring, and I was amazed. The funny part about the story was the fact that the coffee cup I normally used for a cup measurement was proportionately larger as well. So I had been using equivalent measuring tools with just larger results. A great lesson in the technical aspects of cooking.

Over the years, I have been blessed with exposure by travel to many different regions within our country, Canada, and Europe. Embarking on an independent trip meant exploring different cultures and customs through regional markets, home kitchens, cooking schools, and restaurants. I have eagerly returned home to my own kitchen armed with notes and new ingredients, so enjoying the process and possibilities of culinary discovery. Each experiment or replication of an enjoyable dish has meant keeping copious notes and recipes, of which I have enough to fill many books.

Sharing food and talents with my family and friends is one of my life's greatest pleasures. I truly believe "life is in the details", and good food to be the celebration of the good life. Organizing my kitchen to work efficiently is essential. Keeping my pantry stocked so I can easily prepare an impromptu dinner for 6 is a priority. Having common sense references and recipes accessible is priceless.

I believe you will enjoy using this book as a realistic, practical tool. The photographs were taken of actual food prepared in the photo studio kitchen. They were not re-styled or edited as in 99% of most other cookbooks. Why? I wanted your recipe results to be at least as nice as the photos. The recipes are basic recipes: using no mixes and leaving all the preservatives at the supermarket. They are organized and clear, with detailed instructions. I encourage you to read a recipe all the way through before you start, checking the ingredient list, pan sizes and preparation method. Buy the best quality ingredients you can find and afford. They're still only a fraction of a take-out or dining costs.

Your kitchen is your room of inspiration to create a balance of flavors, colors, and textures. Taste as you go. Touch the food. You'll learn how it feels when it's done just right. Listen to the sizzle of the steak, and smell the aroma of your home baked breads.

Transform food and its enjoyment into a deep and memorable experience. Get out of your car and into the kitchen. Sit down with your family to enjoy a dinner you've prepared together. Life is an interactive experience. Live on the edge.

# COOKING
## WITH
# CONFIDENCE

*Inspirations for Good Food at Home*

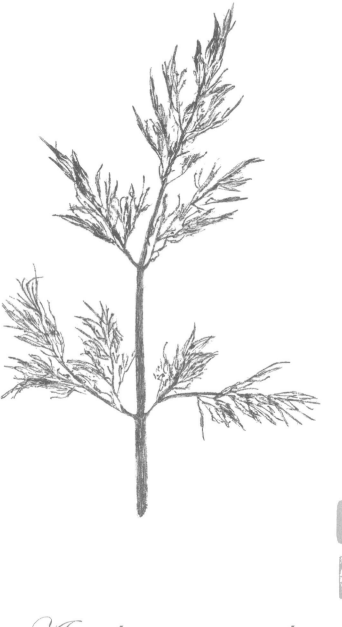

*Anethum graveolens*

*(dill)*

# Starters, Snacks, and Beverages

Amaretto Cheese and Fruit
Artichoke Crostini
Asian Chicken Wings
Basil Tomato Cheese Spread
Blue Cheese Bacon Dip
Corn and Black Bean Salsa
Crab and Crackers
Crackers: Parmesan; Asiago/Cheddar
Hot Wings with Blue Cheese
Party Time Meatballs
Salmon Cracker Spread
Scallop Seviche
Scallops Supreme
Seafood Delights

Hot Drinks/Cold Drinks:
Hot Buttered Rum
Mulled Apple Cider
Apple Brandies
Apple Runners
Lemonade for Real
Strawberry Lemonade Sparklers

Scoops of Confidence

# Amaretto Cheese and Fruit

*An interesting combination of tastes and textures: tart, sweet, creamy, and crunchy, and a perfectly pretty plate for your buffet table.*

**1 (8-ounce) package cream cheese, softened**
**1/4 cup amaretto liqueur**
**1 (2 1/2-ounce) package slivered almonds**

**Fresh apples, unpeeled (2 or 3)**
**Fresh pears, unpeeled (2 or 3)**
**1 cup pineapple juice**

Stir amaretto into the softened cream cheese; whip with a fork to a smooth consistency. Form the mixture into a ball. Cover with plastic wrap and chill until firm. When ready to serve, remove the plastic wrap and press almonds firmly into the cheese ball. Allow cheese to reach room temperature.

Core apples and pears; slice thin. Place slices of fruit in a bowl. Add pineapple juice and stir, coating all of the slices. (This will prevent the fruit from turning brown).

To serve, place cheese ball (accompanied by a small knife for spreading) in the center of a large plate. Arrange fruit slices in a circular fashion surrounding the cheese.

# Artichoke Crostini

*Makes about 4 dozen*

*Crostini means "little toasts". They are easy to make and versatile as well.*

## Crostini:
1 French baguette
extra virgin olive oil

## Artichoke spread:
1 (14-ounce) can artichoke hearts, drained and coarsely chopped
1 (3-ounce) package cream cheese, softened
1/2 cup mayonnaise
1 cup fresh spinach, chopped
2 tablespoons green onions, sliced
2 tablespoons Dijon mustard
2 teaspoons Worcestershire sauce
1 teaspoon dried dill weed
1/2 teaspoon celery salt
1/2 teaspoon bottled hot sauce
1/4 teaspoon ground white pepper
1 cup Parmesan cheese, freshly grated
2 fresh tomatoes, seeded and diced

For crostini, preheat oven to 400 degrees. Cut baguette into 1/4-inch slices; brush both sides with a small amount of oil. Bake 8 minutes or until lightly browned; turn over, and bake additional 8 minutes. Cool.

For artichoke spread, preheat oven to 350 degrees. Butter an 8 x 8-inch baking dish; set aside.

Combine artichokes, cream cheese and mayonnaise in a medium bowl; stir to mix well. Add spinach, onions, mustard, Worcestershire sauce, dill weed, celery salt, hot sauce, and pepper; stir to mix well. Spoon into prepared baking dish. Top with Parmesan cheese and diced tomatoes. Bake 20-25 minutes. Spread on crostini or crackers while still warm, or at room temperature.

COOKING with CONFIDENCE

# Asian Chicken Wings

*Anyone who likes chicken will like these. The recipe easily doubles for a party. Just remember to allow advance prep time for the marinating process.*

**3 pounds fresh chicken wings**

*Marinade:*
**1/3 cup low sodium soy sauce**
**3 tablespoons granulated sugar**
**3 tablespoons brown sugar**
**3 tablespoons rice vinegar**
**1 teaspoon ground ginger (or 1 tablespoon fresh ginger, minced)**
**2 cloves fresh garlic, minced**

Cut the tips from the wings at the joint if desired; discard. If you wish to have smaller pieces, cut the remaining piece at the joint as well. Rinse thoroughly and pat dry. Place the chicken pieces in a heavy duty plastic bag.

For marinade, whisk soy sauce, sugars, vinegar, ginger, and garlic together until sugars are dissolved. Pour over wings. Remove as much air as possible from the bag, close tightly, and refrigerate for 3-6 hours.

Preheat oven to 350 degrees. Line a baking sheet with foil; coat with non-stick spray. Remove wings from bag and place on prepared pan. Bake 1 hour; serve hot.

# Basil Tomato Cheese Spread

*Makes 2 cups*

*You will love this flavor combination of 4 cheeses with deep, rich, sun dried tomatoes.*

2 cups fresh basil
3 cloves fresh garlic
1/2 cup pine nuts, toasted*
1/2 cup sun dried tomatoes in oil, drained
2 tablespoons extra virgin olive oil
4 ounces goat cheese, softened
1/4 cup Asiago cheese, grated
1 1/2 cups Parmesan cheese, grated
1 (8-ounce) package cream cheese, softened
1/4 teaspoon kosher salt
1/4 teaspoon coarsely ground black pepper
1/4 teaspoon thyme
Fresh parsley or chives for garnish, minced

\*       To toast pine nuts, preheat oven to 325 degrees. Place nuts on a baking sheet; bake 10-12 minutes
        or until light brown. Watch carefully, as they burn quickly.

Place basil, garlic, pine nuts, tomatoes, and oil in food processor bowl; pulse several times until mixture is smooth. Remove mixture from processor to a mixing bowl.

Add cheeses, salt, pepper, and thyme; mix well. Cover with plastic wrap; refrigerate.

When ready to serve, bring mixture to room temperature. Spread a thin layer on slices of French bread, olive bread, or crostini. Top with a sprinkling of parsley or chives.

COOKING WITH CONFIDENCE

# Blue Cheese Bacon Dip

*12-15 servings*

*If you love blue cheese........*

8 slices bacon
2 cloves fresh garlic, finely minced
1 (8-ounce) package cream cheese, softened
1/4 cup light cream
4 ounces blue cheese, crumbled
1 teaspoon Worcestershire sauce
1/2 teaspoon bottled hot sauce
1/4 teaspoon dried thyme
2 tablespoons fresh chives, finely chopped
1/4 cup smoked almonds, finely chopped

Preheat oven to 350 degrees.

Fry the bacon until crisp; transfer to a paper towel to drain. Remove all but a trace of fat from the pan; add garlic, cook and stir for 1 minute. Combine softened cream cheese and cream in a deep mixing bowl; beat until smooth. Crumble the bacon and add to the cream cheese mixture. Stir in garlic, blue cheese, Worcestershire sauce, hot sauce, thyme, and chives.

Spoon mixture into a shallow baking/serving dish. Distribute smoked almonds evenly over the top. Bake, uncovered, for 30 minutes. Serve with fresh vegetables, crackers, or crostini.

# Corn and Black Bean Salsa

*Makes 4 cups*

*Food of the summer gods....Great with regular or scoop-shaped tortilla chips.*

1 (15-ounce) can black beans, rinsed and drained
1 1/2 cups corn (fresh and cooked or, if frozen, thawed and cooked)
1/2 cup fresh cilantro, minced
1/4 cup red bell pepper, chopped
1/4 cup red onions, minced
1/4 cup green onions, sliced very thin
1 1/2 teaspoons pickled jalapeno pepper, seeded and minced
1/3 cup fresh lime juice
1/3 cup vegetable oil
1 1/2 teaspoon ground cumin
1/4 teaspoon kosher salt
1/4 teaspoon freshly ground black pepper
3/4 cup fresh tomatoes, seeded and chopped

Combine beans and corn in a medium bowl. Add cilantro, red pepper, onions, and jalapeno pepper; mix well. In a separate bowl, combine lime juice, oil, cumin, salt, and black pepper; whisk to blend well.

Add the lime juice mixture to the corn and onion mixture; stir well.  Gently stir in the chopped tomatoes.

Cover bowl tightly with plastic wrap. Refrigerate at least 3 hours to allow flavors to blend.

# Crab and Crackers

*8-10 appetizer servings*

*Here's a quick-to-fix version of an old favorite. Served warm (as a dip), or cold (as a spread), you'll agree the taste is always on the money. Choose whole wheat or other hearty crackers to showcase this appetizer.*

**1 (8-ounce) cream cheese, softened**
**1/2 cup sour cream**
**1/4 cup mayonnaise**
**1 (6-ounce) can crab meat, drained**
**1/2 cup fresh parsley, minced**
**2 tablespoons onion, grated**
**2 large cloves fresh garlic, minced**
**2 tablespoons sherry or white wine**
**1 tablespoon Dijon mustard**
**1/4 teaspoon Old Bay seasoning**
**1/4 teaspoon bottled hot sauce**
**1/2 cup slivered almonds**
**crackers for serving**

Preheat oven to 325 degrees.

In a large bowl, combine cream cheese, sour cream, and mayonnaise until mixture is fairly smooth and creamy. Stir in crab meat, parsley, onion, garlic, sherry, mustard, Old Bay, and hot sauce; mix well.

Spoon mixture into a shallow 1-quart baking/serving dish. Sprinkle almonds evenly over the top.

Bake 20 minutes. Turn your oven control from "Bake" to "Broil". Move the dish to the uppermost rack of the oven; broil 2 minutes to brown the almonds. Serve (at any chosen temperature) with your favorite crackers as a dip or spread.

# Parmesan Crackers

Makes about 3 dozen

*Easy to make. Dough can also be baked in sheets, and broken into pieces to serve.*

**1 cup finely grated Parmesan cheese**
**1/2 cup butter, softened**
**1 1/2 cups all-purpose flour**
**1/4 teaspoon each: seasoned salt, garlic salt, and dried parsley**
**1/4 teaspoon each: cream of tartar, and baking soda**
**1/3 cup water**

Combine cheese, butter, flour, salts, parsley, cream of tartar, and soda; mix well. Stir in water; mix until dough becomes smooth. Form into a ball; cover with plastic wrap. Refrigerate for 30 minutes.

Preheat oven to 400 degrees. Divide dough into 2 portions. On a lightly floured surface, roll dough as thin as possible. Cut into 2-inch rounds; place on an ungreased baking sheet. Bake 8-10 minutes or until golden brown. Transfer crackers to a wire rack to cool.

# Asiago Cheddar Crackers

Makes about 4 dozen

*You will love the taste - wonderful for snacking all by themselves.*

**1 cup grated Asiago cheese, warmed to room temperature**
**1 cup grated sharp cheddar cheese, warmed to room temperature**
**1/2 cup butter, softened**
**1/4 cup fresh parsley, minced**
**1 1/2 cups all-purpose flour**
**1/4 teaspoon kosher salt**
**1/4 teaspoon cayenne pepper**

Combine cheeses and softened butter in a large bowl; beat until well mixed. Stir in parsley. Add flour, salt, and pepper; stir until a soft dough forms. Divide dough in two equal sized portions; gently form into 2 round "log" shapes. Cover the rolls with plastic wrap; chill for 45 minutes.

Preheat oven to 375 degrees. Slice each log into 1/4-inch pieces and place on ungreased baking sheet. Bake about 15 minutes until crackers are light golden brown. Transfer crackers to a wire rack to cool.

# Hot Wings with Blue Cheese

6-8 appetizer servings

*Easier to make than they look.*

**4 pounds chicken wings (about 24)**
**4 cups vegetable oil for frying**

*First Coating:*
**1 egg, 1 cup milk**

*Second Coating:*
**1 cup all-purpose flour, 2 teaspoons kosher salt, 1/2 teaspoon freshly ground black pepper, 1/4 teaspoon cayenne pepper**

*Blue Cheese Sauce:*

| | |
|---|---|
| **4 ounces blue cheese, crumbled** | **1/4 cup buttermilk** |
| **1/2 cup mayonnaise** | **1/2 cup sour cream** |
| **1 large clove garlic, minced** | **2 teaspoons Worcestershire sauce** |
| **2 tablespoons lemon juice** | **1/2 teaspoon freshly ground black pepper** |

*Dipping Sauce:*
**2 tablespoons melted butter, 1/3 cup bottled hot sauce, 1/4 teaspoon freshly ground black pepper, 1/4 teaspoon garlic powder**

Make the Blue Cheese Sauce first: Whisk blue cheese, buttermilk, mayonnaise, sour cream, garlic, Worcestershire sauce, lemon juice, and pepper in a medium bowl until well mixed. Cover tightly; refrigerate to allow flavors to blend.

For the Dipping Sauce, combine melted butter, hot sauce, black pepper, and garlic powder. Taste; add hot sauce and cayenne pepper if you prefer this a bit "warmer". Set prepared sauce aside.

Preheat oven to 400 degrees. Cut chicken wings at the first joint; discard tips. Wash wings thoroughly and pat dry with paper towels. Heat oil to 380 degrees in a deep, heavy duty skillet or Dutch oven. Mix egg and milk together for the first coating; set aside. Mix flour, salt, and peppers together for the second coating; set aside. Dip wings into egg mixture and then into the flour mixture. Fry in hot oil 5-6 minutes until brown. Remove from oil with a slotted spoon; drain on paper towels. Transfer to a broiler pan; bake in preheated oven for 10 minutes. Coat with Dipping Sauce; serve with Blue Cheese Sauce.

# Party Time Meatballs

*Makes about 50*

*Okay, here it is…A most requested recipe from my kitchen to yours. This recipe easily adapts to a regular meat main dish by replacing the topping with regular barbeque sauce or a gravy. And a bonus idea? Note the option for a Mozzarella Meatball Sandwich.*

## Meatballs:
1 pound lean ground beef
1 pound ground pork
2 eggs
1/2 cup onion, finely chopped
2 cups dry bread crumbs
2 tablespoons dried parsley
1 1/2 teaspoons kosher salt
1/2 teaspoon freshly ground black pepper
1 1/2 teaspoons dried thyme

## Topping:
1 cup apricot preserves
1 cup prepared barbeque sauce of your choice

Preheat oven to 350 degrees. Line a large baking pan with foil; coat lightly with non-stick vegetable spray.

In a large bowl, combine beef, pork, eggs, and onion. In a smaller bowl, combine bread crumbs, parsley, salt, pepper, and thyme; mix thoroughly. Add the bread crumb mixture to the meat and egg mixture; mix lightly to combine all ingredients. Shape into balls (a 1 1/2-inch scoop works well to achieve even-sized portions).

Place meatballs on foil-lined baking pan. For the topping, combine preserves and barbeque sauce; spoon over meatballs. Bake 30-40 minutes or until meatballs are brown and firm. Serve warm.

**MOZZARELLA MEATBALL SANDWICH**: Slice a few meatballs in half and place on a kaiser roll; top with a spoonful of sauce and a slice of mozzarella cheese. Bake 3-5 minutes at 350 degrees until cheese melts.

COOKING WITH CONFIDENCE

# Salmon Cracker Spread

*Serves 10-12*

*An easy, do-ahead crowd pleaser.*

1 (16-ounce) can red salmon
1 (8-ounce) package cream cheese, softened
1/4 cup onion, diced
1 1/2 teaspoons bottled horseradish
1 teaspoon liquid smoke
2 teaspoons fresh chives (regular or garlic), finely chopped
1 lemon, thinly sliced

Drain salmon. Remove bones and skin; flake gently with a fork. Mix with cream cheese, onion, horseradish, liquid smoke, and chives. Place in shallow serving dish; cover, and refrigerate overnight. To serve, bring to room temperature; garnish with lemon slices. Serve with hearty, whole wheat crackers.

# Scallops Seviche

*A wonderful fix-it-and-forget-it appetizer. If purchasing frozen scallops, buy the flash frozen ones called dry scallops which have had no preservatives added.*

**1 pound bay scallops (these are the small ones)**

*Marinade:*
**2 cups white wine vinegar**
**1/4 cup honey**
**2 tablespoons onion, finely chopped**
**1 tablespoon dried tarragon**
**1 teaspoon dried basil**
**1 teaspoon kosher salt**
**3/4 teaspoon freshly ground black pepper**
**1/4 teaspoon dried marjoram**
**1/4 teaspoon dried dill weed**
**1 large clove garlic, finely chopped**
**3/4 cup extra virgin olive oil**
**2 avocados, peeled and sliced thinly.**

Rinse and pat scallops completely dry with a paper towel; set aside.

For marinade, whisk vinegar and honey together in a small bowl until dissolved. Add onion, tarragon, basil, salt, pepper, marjoram, dill, garlic, and olive oil; whisk again until well mixed.

Place scallops in a shallow glass dish. Add marinade; stir well. Drizzle oil over the top. Cover the dish tightly; refrigerate at least 8 hours, stirring occasionally. The acidity of the vinegar actually "cooks" the scallops during this process.

To serve, drain the scallops; spoon onto a serving plate lined with avocado slices.

# Scallops Supreme

*4 servings*

*An impressive looking, yet easy-to-make treat. Prepare the sauce in advance, and you can be ready to serve these in 10 minutes.*

**1 pound (about 10) fresh jumbo sea scallops, or dry frozen scallops, thawed**
**1/2 cup stone ground corn meal**
**1/2 cup all-purpose flour**
**1 tablespoon Old Bay seasoning**
**1/2 teaspoon freshly ground black pepper**
**2 tablespoons clarified butter**
**2 tablespoons canola oil**

*Sauce:*
**2 tablespoons clarified butter**
**1 tablespoon canola oil**
**2 tablespoons shallots, minced**
**2 cloves fresh garlic, minced**
**3/4 cup dry white wine**
**2/3 cup heavy cream**
**1 1/2 teaspoons tomato paste**
**1/2 teaspoon instant chicken bouillon granules**
**1/2 teaspoon Old Bay seasoning**
**1/2 teaspoon dried dill weed**
**1/4 teaspoon bottled hot sauce**
**1 tablespoon freeze dried or fresh basil, finely chopped**
**2 tablespoons green onion, minced**
**1 1/2 cups tomatoes, seeded and finely diced**

Prepare sauce first: Stir butter and oil together in a skillet over medium heat. Add shallots; cook and stir 1 minute. Add garlic; cook an additional minute. Reduce heat to medium low. Stir in wine; cook 4 minutes to reduce in volume. Whisk in cream, tomato paste, bouillon, Old Bay, dill weed, and hot sauce; simmer for 2 minutes. Stir in basil, green onions, and tomatoes.

To prepare scallops, remove connective tissue from the side of each; pat dry. Slice in half horizontally. Stir corn meal, flour, Old Bay, and pepper together in a shallow dish. Dredge each scallop in the flour mixture; set aside for about 5 minutes. Combine clarified butter and oil in a large, heavy skillet over medium high heat. Add scallops and cook for just a minute or so until golden brown. Turn over to cook the other side. The scallops are not thick; take care not to overcook. To serve, spoon warm sauce onto a small plate, along with 5 scallop halves.

# Seafood Delights

*Makes about 4 cups*

*Fresh and flavorful.*

1 pound medium shrimp, cooked and cooled
1 pound crabmeat, cooked and flaked
1 cup finely chopped celery
3/4 cup finely sliced green onions
1 teaspoon dill weed
1/2 teaspoon Old Bay seasoning
1/4 teaspoon freshly ground pepper
1/4 cup extra virgin olive oil
1/2 cup freshly squeezed lemon juice

In a large glass mixing bowl, combine all ingredients.  Cover with plastic wrap; refrigerate at least 4 hours to allow flavors to blend. Serve on crisp crackers or in phyllo puffed pastry shells.

# Hot Drinks, Cold Drinks

## Hot Buttered Rum Mix

For 25 servings: Combine 2 cups brown sugar (packed), 1 cup softened butter, 1 egg, 1/2 tablespoon each of cinnamon and allspice, 1/2 teaspoon each of cloves and nutmeg. Beat with an electric mixer for 30 minutes, scraping down sides of bowl often. Place in an airtight container; refrigerate. For 1 cup: 1 tablespoon of mix, 1 ounce rum or brandy (or 1/2 ounce of each), and enough very hot water to fill the cup. Stir briskly. Any leftover mix can be covered tightly and refrigerated.

## Mulled Apple Cider

Simmer 2 quarts apple juice or cider, 3 whole cloves, 3 whole allspice, and 1 teaspoon ground nutmeg for 10 minutes. Add 1/3 cup frozen orange juice concentrate, 1/3 cup frozen lemonade concentrate, and 1/2 cup brown sugar. Bring to a simmer; serve hot.

## Apple Brandies

For 4 servings: Heat 4 cups mulled apple cider until simmering. Whip 1/2 cup heavy cream with 1 tablespoon confectioners' sugar and 1/4 cup good quality apple brandy. Grind 2 whole cloves and 2 whole allspice together. To serve, pour hot cider into cups. Top with a dollop of flavored whipped cream and sprinkle with spices. Garnish with a cinnamon stick.

## Apple Runners

For 2 servings: In a small saucepan, make sweet and sour syrup by bringing 1 cup water, 1 cup lemon juice concentrate, and 1 cup granulated sugar to a boil over medium heat, stirring until sugar dissolves. To serve, pour 2 ounces apple brandy and 1 ounce sweet and sour syrup into a short glass. Add 1 ounce very hot water; stir briskly.

## Lemonade for Real

For 2 quarts: Grate the lemon rind from 2 lemons. In a medium saucepan, bring 2 cups water, 2 cups granulated sugar and lemon rind to a boil over medium heat, stirring to dissolve sugar. Remove from heat; cover, and let steep 15 minutes, allowing flavors to blend. To serve, pour syrup into a 2-quart pitcher. Add 2 cups freshly squeezed lemon juice (from about 10-12 lemons), 3 cups cold water, and a few chopped lemon rinds; stir well. Serve over ice; garnish with lemon slices.

## Strawberry Lemonade Sparkler

For 8 servings: In a small saucepan, bring 3/4 cup granulated sugar, 1 cup water, and 1/3 cup fresh mint leaves to a boil over medium heat, stirring to dissolve sugar. Remove from heat, cover, and let steep 15 minutes, allowing flavors to blend. Strain to remove mint; allow to cool another 10 minutes. Puree strawberries and 2 tablespoons granulated sugar until smooth. Combine strawberry puree and lemon juice in a 1 1/2-quart container. Stir in mint syrup; refrigerate. When ready to serve, divide mixture between 8 champagne glasses. Top with soda water or wine.

# Scoops of Confidence
## For Starters, Snacks, and Beverages

If entertaining at regular mealtime, estimate 10-12 substantial **appetizers per person**. If hosting a cocktail party before serving dinner, present a lighter fare (5-6 pieces per person). Always plan generously. You can't control appetites - especially for good food. Coordinate your appetizers with your dinner fare in terms of form, texture, and flavor.

**Plan** enough time and oven space to finish your appetizers, and use a timer - it's easy to become distracted when there's activity in the kitchen.

Before entertaining any new friends, check with them regarding any **food allergies**. Peanuts and shellfish are two of the usual suspects. Always know what's in your food.

Let your food and setting be the focus. When serving **buffet-style,** physically raise the level of your food using pedestals, boxes or even garden urns (think wide and sturdy). Positioning food at varying heights creates visual interest, and is very comfortable for guests serving themselves.

Eliminate the potential for a "reach across" accident by keeping any candles at a higher elevation than (and away from) your serving platters.

Remember: food presents itself more dramatically on plain dishes with no pattern. Too many colors and too many patterns confuse the eye.

Flavors of **garnishes** should complement, not overpower, your appetizers… and be totally edible so guests don't have to worry about discarding them. If using herbs, keep them fresh by re-cutting their stems and placing the bunch in a glass, water-filled container. Cover with a plastic bag, and refrigerate until needed.

Cutting **green onions** and/or fresh chives at an extreme angle produces beautifully shaped and interesting looking "rings" for garnishing.

*Salvia officinalis*

(Sage)

BREAKFAST    BRUNCHES    BREADS

# Breakfast, Brunches, Breads

Brunch Souffle
Fresh Tomato Tart
Pizza Quiche
Sausage and Hashbrown Egg Bake
Triple Cheese Strata

Pancake and Waffle Syrups
Perfect Pancakes
Potato Pancakes
Stuffed French Toast

Baking Powder Biscuits
Buttermilk Doughnuts
Focaccia Sandwiches
Herbed Focaccia
Lemon Scones
Norwegian Lefse
Popovers
Yankee Cornbread

Cherry Bread
Cranberry Bread
Easy Banana Bread
Lemon Tea Bread
Pumpkin Bread
Rhubarb Quick Bread

Apple Pecan Muffins
Banana Chocolate Chip Muffins
Corn Muffins
French Apple Muffins
Morning Glory Muffins
Orange Muffins
Strawberry Muffins
Triple Chocolate Muffins

Scoops of Confidence

COOKING WITH CONFIDENCE

# Brunch Souffle

*A great dish to start a lazy afternoon.*

**10 slices bacon, diced**
**1 tablespoon butter**
**8 ounces fresh mushrooms, sliced**
**1/4 cup green onions, thinly sliced**
**2 (3-ounce) packages dried beef - rinsed, dried, and diced**
**1/2 cup all-purpose flour**
**1/4 teaspoon freshly ground pepper**
**4 cups milk**
**1 tablespoon parsley, chopped**
**1/4 teaspoon bottled hot sauce**
**4 tablespoons butter**
**12 eggs, slightly beaten**
**3/4 cup light cream**
**1/4 teaspoon kosher salt**

Preheat oven to 350 degrees. Generously butter a 9-inch souffle dish; set aside.

Cook bacon in a medium skillet until brown and crisp; transfer to a paper towel to drain. Retaining about 1 tablespoon bacon drippings and adding 1 tablespoon butter, return skillet to the heat. Add mushrooms; cook and stir for about 2-3 minutes until slightly browned. Remove about 1/2 cup of the mushrooms and set aside for garnish. Add onions, dried beef, and reserved bacon pieces to the skillet; mix well. Stir in flour and pepper. Slowly add milk, stirring and cooking until sauce is thick and smooth. Add parsley and hot sauce. Remove from heat, cover, and set aside.

In a medium skillet, melt butter. Add beaten eggs, cream, and salt; cook and stir until eggs are softly scrambled and still quite moist.

Layer half of the scrambled eggs in prepared souffle dish, then spoon half of the sauce over the eggs. Repeat procedure, using all remaining eggs and sauce. Top with reserved mushrooms.

Bake 20 minutes. Serve immediately.

BREAKFAST BRUNCHES BREADS 35

# Fresh Tomato Tart

*8 servings*

*Served in smaller portions, this tart also makes a delicious appetizer.*

3 large tomatoes, cut into 1/2-inch slices, seeds removed
1 1/2 cups flour
1/2 teaspoon kosher salt
1/4 cup unsalted butter, chilled and cut into small pieces
3-4 tablespoons ice cold water
2 tablespoons Dijon mustard
3 tablespoons chopped fresh basil
4 ounces mozzarella cheese, grated
2 eggs
1 cup heavy cream
1/2 teaspoon freshly ground pepper

Place tomatoes in a colander to drain for 30 minutes. Pat dry with paper towels. Set aside.

Mix flour and salt; add butter and mix with a pastry blender until very crumbly. Add water one tablespoon at a time, mixing thoroughly with a fork after each addition. Turn out onto a lightly floured surface; roll to fit a 10-inch round or rectangular tart pan. Fit pastry into pan, trimming the excess to about 1/2-inch larger than the pan. Fold the overhanging pastry back into the pan; press well into the sides and raise the edge of the pastry just a little above the sides to allow for shrinkage during baking. Transfer the pastry filled pan to the freezer for 20 minutes. Time in the freezer will allow the dough to relax, resulting in a more tender crust.

Using a spatula, spread mustard over frozen pastry. Sprinkle with basil and cheese. For the next layer, place the tomato slices very close together to totally cover the surface. Beat eggs, cream, and pepper until well blended; pour this mixture over the layer of tomatoes.

Bake 30 minutes; cool 10 minutes before slicing into wedges or squares. Serve warm.

COOKING WITH CONFIDENCE

# Pizza Quiche

*The no-roll pastry speeds up assembly.*

1 1/2 cups all-purpose flour
1 1/2 teaspoons granulated sugar
3/4 teaspoon kosher salt
1/4 cup plus 1 tablespoon canola oil
2 tablespoons milk
4 eggs
1 cup pizza sauce (or salsa, or picante sauce)
1 cup pepperoni, diced
2 1/2 cups sharp cheddar cheese, shredded (about 1/2 pound)
1 1/2 cups mozzarella cheese, shredded
1 cup Parmesan cheese, shredded
1 tablespoon parsley for garnish

Preheat oven to 400 degrees.

Stir flour, sugar, and salt together in a 10-inch pie plate. Whisk oil and milk in a small bowl. Add the oil mixture to the flour mixture; toss with a fork until moist and crumbly. Press pastry crumbs evenly into bottom and up the sides of the pie plate. Bake for 5 minutes. Remove from oven, and reduce oven temperature to 350 degrees.

In a medium bowl, beat eggs until thick and frothy. Stir in pizza sauce and pepperoni; set aside. Combine all three varieties of cheese, and spoon about half of this over the baked crust. Pour egg mixture over the cheese, add the remaining cheese, and top with a sprinkling of parsley.

Bake 45 minutes or until knife inserted in the center of the quiche comes out clean. Sometimes oil from the pepperoni collects on the top of the quiche. If this happens, remove with a light touch of a paper towel. Allow quiche to rest 10 minutes before cutting into wedges. Serve hot.

# Sausage and Hashbrown Egg Bake

*12 servings*

*This layered breakfast dish is a favorite of my sister Marilyn. She loves to take this dish on camping trips. It's an easy do-ahead dish easily halved for a smaller gathering.*

**4 cups frozen hashbrown potatoes, thawed and well drained***
**2 (12 ounce) packages breakfast sausage - hot or mild**
**1 1/2 cups grated cheddar cheese**
**1 cup grated Swiss cheese**
**1 cup grated pepper jack cheese**
**8 eggs**
**2 cups half and half**
**1 1/2 cups milk**
**1/2 cup onions, finely diced**
**1 1/2 teaspoons prepared mustard**
**1/4 teaspoon kosher salt**
**1/8 teaspoon freshly ground pepper**

Butter a 9 x 13-inch baking pan. In a large skillet, cook and stir sausage until browned; drain and set aside. Distribute the hashbrowns evenly over the bottom of the pan. Sprinkle the grated cheddar, swiss, and pepper jack cheeses over the hashbrowns. Layer the browned sausage over the cheeses.

In a large bowl, beat eggs. Add half and half, milk, onions, mustard, salt, and pepper; mix well. Pour the egg mixture over the mixture in the pan. Cover the pan tightly; refrigerate overnight.

Preheat oven to 325 degrees. Remove egg bake from the refrigerator. Bake, uncovered, for 40 minutes. Let stand for 15 minutes before cutting in squares to serve.

\*      Ice crystals form when potatoes are frozen for any length of time. Make sure they are completely thawed, drained, and patted dry.

COOKING WITH CONFIDENCE

# Triple Cheese Strata

*Assembling this dish the night before will simplify your morning. Lovely served with fresh fruit.*

**French bread, cubed (about 1/2 of a 1 pound loaf)**
**2 cups Swiss cheese, shredded**
**1 cup Monterey Jack cheese, shredded**
**2 cups ham, diced**
**3 green onions, sliced**
**6 eggs**
**2 cups milk**
**1/4 cup dry white wine**
**2 teaspoons Dijon mustard**
**1/4 teaspoon kosher salt**
**1/4 teaspoon freshly ground black pepper**
**2 tablespoons fresh chives**

*Sauce for topping:*
**1 cup sour cream**
**1/2 cup grated Parmesan cheese**
**1/8 teaspoon kosher salt**
**1/8 teaspoon freshly ground black pepper**

Place bread cubes in a 9 1/2 x 13 1/2-inch greased baking dish. Top with Swiss and Monterey Jack cheeses, ham, and green onions. Combine eggs, milk, wine, mustard, salt, and pepper in a large mixing bowl; beat well. Pour egg mixture over the bread cube mixture in the baking dish. Press lightly to allow liquid to absorb. Sprinkle with fresh chives. Cover with plastic wrap; transfer to refrigerator to chill 4-24 hours. Allow to return to room temperature before baking.

Preheat oven to 325 degrees. Cover baking dish with foil; bake 40-45 minutes until puffed, and knife inserted in the center comes out clean. Let rest 10 minutes.

Combine sour cream, Parmesan cheese, salt, and pepper in a small saucepan. Stir over low heat until warmed.

To serve, cut strata into equal pieces; top with a spoonful of sauce.

# Pancake and Waffle Syrups

*Here are three easy-to-make syrups you'll love and enjoy. Nice changes from the traditional maple flavor, the Orange and Cinnamon Cream are best served warm and the Blueberry is good warm or cold.*

## Orange Syrup

**1/4 cup frozen orange juice concentrate**
**1/4 cup light corn syrup**
**1/3 cup granulated sugar**
**2 tablespoons butter**

Combine orange juice concentrate, corn syrup, sugar and butter in a small saucepan. Simmer 5 minutes, stirring occasionally.

## Blueberry Syrup

**2 cups fresh berries, mashed**
**2/3 cup granulated sugar**
**1 1/2 teaspoons grated lemon peel**
**1 teaspoon fresh lemon juice**
**1/3 cup water**

Combine blueberries, sugar, peel, juice, and water in a saucepan. Cook and stir until sugar dissolves. Simmer 8 minutes. Strain and serve.

## Cinnamon Cream Syrup

**1/2 cup granulated sugar**
**1 tablespoon cornstarch**
**1/2 cup dark corn syrup**
**1/2 cup heavy cream**
**2 tablespoons butter**
**1/8 teaspoon cinnamon**
**1 cup raisins**

Combine sugar and cornstarch in saucepan. Add corn syrup, cream, butter, cinnamon, and raisins. Simmer for 5 minutes, stirring occasionally.

COOKING WITH CONFIDENCE

# Perfect Pancakes

*Makes 12 pancakes*

*If you've only made pancakes from a mix, try these. So easy, so quick, so good, and no preservatives. Even the guys at the cabin make them. Check out the variations for Blueberry and Banana.*

**3 eggs**
**2 1/2 cups low fat buttermilk**
**2 tablespoons butter, melted**
**2 teaspoons granulated sugar**
**2 cups all-purpose flour**
**1 teaspoon baking soda**
**1 teaspoon baking powder**
**1/2 teaspoon kosher salt**

Preheat a griddle to 375 degrees. If you're using a stovetop skillet, make your batter before heating the pan.

Separate egg yolks from the whites, placing the yolks in a large bowl and the whites in a small, deep bowl. Beat the egg whites until stiff peaks form; set aside.

Add buttermilk, butter, and sugar to the egg yolks; beat well. Stir in flour, sugar, soda, baking powder, and salt. Do not overmix - a few lumps are all right. If you need to heat a skillet, do it as this time.

Gently fold in beaten egg whites, being careful not to overmix. Your batter should be rather fluffy, with some of the egg whites still visible.

Test your griddle or skillet to make sure it's medium hot. (At the right temperature, a few drops of water sprinkled on the surface will sizzle and dance). For each pancake, pour about 1/3 cup batter onto hot griddle and spread into a circle. Flip to cook the second side as soon as pancakes are covered with bubbles and edges are slightly dry. Serve immediately with butter and warm syrup. To serve an entire batch at the same time, cover the pancakes loosely and keep warm in a 200 degree oven.

## Variations:
**BLUEBERRY PANCAKES**: Fold 1 1/2 cups fresh or frozen blueberries into the batter or, to even out distribution, a few berries may be added to each pancake after batter is poured on the griddle.
**BANANA PANCAKES**: Peel and mash 2 large bananas; mix with 1 teaspoon cinnamon. Fold the banana mixture into the batter.

# Potato Pancakes

*Although I don't believe he measured even one of the ingredients, Dad used to make these yummies for the crew. They are excellent served with sausage, applesauce and yogurt.*

**4 cups raw potatoes, peeled and coarsely grated (about 2 pounds)**
**2 eggs**
**1/4 cup milk or light cream**
**1 cup onions, minced**
**1 teaspoon kosher salt**
**1/4 teaspoon coarsely ground black pepper**
**1/2 cup all-purpose flour**
**1/2 teaspoon baking powder**
**canola oil (about 2/3 to 3/4 cup)**

Grate the potatoes into a bowl filled with cold water. (The potatoes won't turn brown and excess starch is removed, resulting in crisper pancakes).

Beat the eggs in a separate bowl. Stir in milk, onions, salt, pepper, flour, and baking powder; mix until smooth. Drain the grated potatoes, carefully squeezing out all the liquid. Add potatoes to the egg mixture; stir well.

Preheat a large skillet with oil (about 1/4-inch deep) to medium hot. Test for the right temperature: a few drops of water sprinkled on the oil should sizzle across the surface. Gently drop mixture into skillet using a 1/4-cup measure, and spread into rounds with a spoon. Brown on one side, about 1 to 1 1/2 minutes, then turn and cook about an additional minute to brown the other side. Drain on paper towels. If you cannot serve immediately, cover loosely and keep warm in a 200 degree oven.

COOKING WITH CONFIDENCE

# Stuffed French Toast

*6 servings*

This is a breakfast treat you will truly love, as it combines bread, fruit, eggs, cream cheese, and a little sugar to get your motor running in the morning.

**1 loaf French bread (firm texture, soft crust)**
**6 eggs**
**1 1/2 cups milk**
**1/2 cup heavy cream**
**2 tablespoons granulated sugar**
**1 1/2 teaspoon pure vanilla extract**
**1/2 teaspoon kosher salt**
**1/2 teaspoon cinnamon**
**1 (8-ounce) package cream cheese, very cold**
**3/4 cup diced fresh strawberries, mixed with 1/2 cup strawberry preserves***
**1/3 cup chopped walnuts (optional)**
**2 tablespoons butter, divided**

Preheat oven to 375 degrees. Place a large baking sheet in the oven to warm.

Cut 6 slices of bread, each about 1 1/4-inch thick. With a small serrated knife, make a horizontal cut in the center of each top crust to form a "pocket". Be careful not to cut all the way through the bottom of the slice. Cut the block of cream cheese into 12 thin slices. Fill the pocket with 1 slice of cream cheese, about 3 tablespoons of filling, 1 more slice of cheese, and a few chopped walnut pieces. Press edges together to close the pocket as tightly as possible. Repeat procedure with remaining bread slices. Place "sandwiches" in a shallow dish or pan large enough to accommodate all six.

Heat 1 tablespoon butter in a skillet. In a medium mixing bowl, beat eggs. Stir in milk, cream, sugar, vanilla, salt, and cinnamon; beat well. Pour egg mixture over the sandwiches; flip them over to drench both sides.

Place 3 of the sandwiches in the hot skillet; cook about 2-3 minutes over medium-high heat until golden brown. Flip over; cook additional minute. Transfer sandwiches to the warm pan in the oven; bake 10 minutes until puffed. Repeat procedure with remaining butter and sandwiches. Serve hot with syrup or topping of your choice.

\*       Choice of fruit fillings is limited only by your imagination. Try fresh peaches with peach preserves, cooked apples with raisins, or any good quality fruited pie filling. Whatever you like with cream cheese works.

# Baking Powder Biscuits

*Makes 10-12*

*The standard biscuits using lemon-lime soda instead of cream. I have made these for many years, and they always turn out great. Split them in half and they work well as a base for fresh strawberry shortcake.*

**2 cups all-purpose flour**
**4 teaspoons baking powder***
**1 teaspoon kosher salt**
**1/2 cup vegetable shortening**
**3/4 cup cold lemon-lime soda**

Preheat oven to 450 degrees.

Whisk the flour, baking powder, and salt together. Using a pastry cutter or fork, cut the shortening into the flour mixture until mixture resembles coarse crumbs. Add lemon-lime soda all at once; stir until just moistened. Turn batter out onto a lightly floured surface. Using a gentle touch, knead just a few times until a soft dough is formed. Pat or roll to a 3/4-inch thickness; cut with a floured 2-inch biscuit cutter.

Transfer biscuits to an ungreased baking sheet. Bake about 10 minutes until tops are an even golden brown. Serve immediately.

*       Make sure your baking powder is fresh. Check the expiration date on the bottom of the can. If it's old, your biscuits will not rise worth a darn.

COOKING WITH CONFIDENCE

# Buttermilk Doughnuts

*Makes about 4 dozen*

*Here is an old fashioned treat and my oldest brother Orvin's favorite food.*

**3 eggs, beaten**
**1 1/4 cups granulated sugar**
**3/4 cup buttermilk**
**1/2 cup heavy cream**
**1 teaspoon pure vanilla extract**
**4 1/2 cups all-purpose flour**
**1 tablespoon baking powder**
**1/2 teaspoon baking soda**
**3/4 teaspoon kosher salt**
**2 teaspoons nutmeg**
**1/4 teaspoon ginger**
**2 tablespoons melted butter**
**5 cups vegetable oil for frying**
**additional flour for rolling and cutting**

In a large mixing bowl combine the beaten eggs, sugar, buttermilk, cream, and vanilla; mix well. In a separate bowl mix flour, baking powder, soda, salt, nutmeg, and ginger. Gradually add the flour mixture to the egg mixture; stir well. Add the melted butter and mix until combined. Mix batter by hand; beating too long with a mixer will make your doughnuts tough. The batter will be rather sticky.

Prepare your work area before continuing. Lightly coat a large baking pan with non-stick vegetable spray; set aside. Place a double layer of paper towel on another large baking pan and place near the stove for your finished doughnuts. Pour oil into a heavy duty Dutch oven or extra deep frying pan. Preheat oil to 375 degrees as measured on an instant read thermometer.

Spoon out a third of the batter onto a floured work surface. Roll out to a uniform 1/2-inch thickness using a well floured rolling pin. Cut the dough with a floured doughnut cutter; transfer cut doughnuts to the pan prepared with non stick spray. Repeat with remaining batter.

Using a slotted spoon, carefully lower 4-5 cut doughnuts into the hot oil. When their edges turn a light brown (about a minute or less), turn the doughnuts over to finish cooking. Remove doughnuts from oil as soon as both sides are browned; transfer onto the towel covered baking sheet to drain and cool. A little practice will make you a doughnut-making expert. Remember: hot oil is extremely dangerous, so use every safety precaution.

# *Focaccia Sandwiches*

*Focaccia, aka Italian flatbread, can be the base for many different varieties of sandwiches. Listed below are a few for you to try. The Magnificent Beefburger has general directions; the remaining list includes various combinations to inspire the chef within. There's nothing you can't pair up with this wonderful bread.*

### <u>Magnificent Beefburger:</u>

This takes the American burger to a whole new level of appreciation and enjoyment. Combine ground chuck with salt, pepper, and Worcestershire sauce. Allow the seasoned beef to rest for 15 minutes so flavors can blend. Form into round patties; grill or panfry.

For sandwich, cut a piece of focaccia large enough to reach beyond the edges of the burger; slice in half horizontally. Spread both pieces of bread with a little mayonnaise or dressing. Stack one slice with greens of your choice, a slice of provolone, the burger, another slice of provolone, 2 grilled portobello mushroom slices, a tomato slice, greens again, and the other piece of focaccia. As soon as the "lid" is on the sandwich, press it down just a bit and secure it with a pick. It's a full meal deal.

### <u>Italian:</u>

Prosciutto, sliced fresh mozzarella, greens, tomato, onions, dressing

### <u>Seacoast:</u>

Shrimp salad, sliced avocado, greens, dressing

### <u>Pepper Beef:</u>

Thinly sliced beef tenderloin, roasted red pepper, red onion, romaine, Caesar dressing

### <u>Farm Salad:</u>

Two kinds of greens, tomato, cucumber, onion, goat cheese, dressing

### <u>Tuscan Grille:</u>

Grilled chicken breast, fresh mozzarella, artichoke hearts, tomato, mixed greens, pesto, mayonnaise

### <u>Veggie:</u>

Marinated carrots, artichokes and broccoli, greens, gorgonzola, dressing

### <u>Bello:</u>

Roasted red pepper, greens, tomato, grilled portobello, goat cheese, dressing

# Herbed Focaccia

*This Italian flatbread has a wonderful taste and texture, absolutely perfect for sandwiches of any kind.*

4 cups bread flour
1 1/2 tsp sugar
1 1/2 tsp kosher salt plus a little more for topping
2 teaspoons rapid rise yeast
2 tablespoons extra virgin olive oil
2/3 cup finely chopped onion
2 cloves finely chopped garlic
1/2 cup pitted black olives, drained and finely chopped
2 tablespoons chopped fresh thyme
3 tablespoons chopped fresh basil
2 teaspoons chopped fresh rosemary
1/2 teaspoon freshly ground black pepper
1 cup water
1 cup milk
1 cup Asiago or Parmesan cheese, grated
1 cup cornmeal for rolling and dusting pan

Combine bread flour, sugar, salt and yeast in a large mixing bowl; set aside. Heat oil in a small skillet. Add onions and garlic; cook and stir over medium heat until tender. Add olives, thyme, basil, rosemary, and pepper. Cook one additional minute; remove from heat.

In a small saucepan, heat water and milk together to 125 degrees; add to herb mixture. Combine reserved flour mixture with herb and milk mixture; stir well. Turn the dough out onto a slightly floured work surface. Wash and dry your mixing bowl; generously coat the inside of the bowl with oil and set aside. Add a small amount of flour to the dough to obtain a soft consistency; knead 4-5 minutes or until smooth and elastic. Transfer dough to the bowl and cover tightly with plastic wrap. Place a towel over the entire bowl; let rise in a warm, draft-free place about 2 hours or until doubled in bulk.

Lightly coat the surface of a 15 x 10 x 1-inch baking pan with non-stick spray. Sprinkle the pan lightly with cornmeal; set aside. Punch dough down and transfer to a work surface lightly coated with cornmeal. Sprinkle dough with grated cheese; knead until well combined. Shape into a large rectangle, and place in prepared pan. Stretch and pat dough to cover entire surface. Let dough rise one additional hour until it looks pillow-like.

Preheat oven to 450 degrees. Using your fingers, make deep indentations 2 inches apart in dough surface. Brush a small amount of olive oil on top and sprinkle with kosher salt. Bake for about 30 minutes until the edges are golden brown and crisp. Transfer focaccia from the pan to a wire rack to cool. Use a serrated knife to cut into desired size pieces. For storage and later use, wrap bread in foil and place inside a plastic bag. Close tightly and refrigerate for up to two days, or double wrap and freeze up to two months. Thaw at room temperature for a few hours; refresh and re-crisp by reheating for a few minutes in a 400 degree oven.

# Lemon Scones

*Nice, refreshing flavor; easy to make. Excellent served warm with honey butter.*

## Scones:
2 cups all-purpose flour
1/4 cup granulated sugar
1 tablespoon baking powder
1/2 teaspoon kosher salt
3/4 cup dried cherries (or substitute any finely chopped dried fruit or raisins)
1 1/2 tablespoons grated fresh lemon peel
1 1/4 cups heavy cream

## Topping:
2 tablespoons butter, melted
1 tablespoon grated fresh lemon peel
2 tablespoons granulated sugar

Preheat oven to 425 degrees.

In a medium mixing bowl, whisk flour, sugar, baking powder, and salt together. Add cherries and lemon peel; mix well. Stir in cream; mix just until a moist and sticky batter forms. Scoop onto a lightly floured surface; use a very gentle touch to knead just 5 or 6 times to pull the dough together. Pat into an 8 or 9-inch round, about 1/2-inch thick. Cut into 12 equal sized wedges; transfer to an ungreased baking sheet.

For topping, brush scones with melted butter. Combine lemon peel and sugar; sprinkle over the top and sides. Bake about 15 minutes until golden brown. Serve warm.

COOKING with CONFIDENCE

# Norwegian Lefse

*Makes about 22 rounds*

*This recipe is from my sister, Lois, who learned how to make lefse when she married a Norwegian. Served as a traditional starch at a Scandinavian holiday dinner, lefse resembles a tortilla, but the taste is very different. It is often spread with softened butter, sprinkled with granulated or brown sugar, rolled up tightly, and eaten by hand.*

**Russet potatoes (about 4 pounds)**
**1/2 cup vegetable oil**
**1/4 cup heavy cream**
**2 tablespoons granulated sugar**
**1 (scant) tablespoon salt**
**2 cups all-purpose flour**

Clean the potatoes, leaving skins intact. Place potatoes in a large saucepan, cover with cold water; cook until fork pierces each easily; drain , and remove skins. Put peeled, warm potatoes through a food mill or ricer; measure the potatoes to equal 6 cups.

Place the riced potatoes in a medium mixing bowl. Stir in oil, cream, sugar, and salt; beat until potatoes have a soft, velvety texture. Place a paper towel over the bowl to absorb moisture, then cover the bowl tightly with plastic wrap. Refrigerate overnight.

To finish, preheat griddle to 475 degrees. Add the flour gradually to the cooled potato mixture until smooth and pliable. Spoon into a 1/4 cup dry measure; remove, and form into 3x 3/4-inch disks; roll into thin rounds. Place on a hot, dry griddle. Grill until bubbles start to rise (about 35 seconds); flip and grill second side until spots are golden brown.  Place on a dampened cotton towel to cool; cover to retain softness. Fold rounds in half, then into quarters. Store in heavy duty plastic bags, in the refrigerator, up to 1 week.

# Popovers

*Makes 6 in a popover pan*

*Many factors affect the outcome of a good popover. Before you get out your whisk, check out the tips and techniques listed at the bottom of this page. Your frequently asked popover questions will be answered.*

**1 1/2 cup all-purpose flour**
**3/4 teaspoon kosher salt**
**3 eggs, lightly beaten**
**1 1/2 cups milk**

Preheat oven to 425 degrees. You will use the center rack so move any rack above that level (popovers are tall). Generously grease a popover pan.

Whisk the flour and salt together; set aside. Whisk eggs slightly. Stir in milk. Add the flour mixture to the egg mixture; whisk until just blended. Divide batter equally to fill the prepared pan.

Bake 35-40 minutes until golden brown and firm to the touch. Serve immediately. Great with butter and homemade strawberry jam.

## Popover Tips:

*   Use only fresh, fresh eggs. It makes a difference.
*   The eggs and milk should be at room temperature when batter is mixed.
*   Go gentle with the batter. If overbeaten, popovers will not raise as high. Don't even think about using a food processor for this task. A hand whisk works just fine.
*   Overcome the urge to open the oven door while the popovers are baking. Drafts make popovers collapse.
*   If you like your popovers dry in the center, pierce them with a sharp knife on one side when they're done to let the steam escape and return them to the oven for a minute or so.
*   Ideally, the batter should fill to about 1/3-inch from the top of your baking container. If you do not have a popover pan and are using custard cups instead, fill only half full.
*   Controversy reigns in the "start with a cold oven" or "preheat the oven" theory. I have tried both, and my vote is for the preheated.

# Yankee Cornbread

*Different from the cornbread traditionally made in the southern states with white cornmeal, this version uses yellow. It has a cake-like texture and tastes a little sweeter than its southern counterpart. If you have a choice, purchase flavorful stone-ground cornmeal rather than the familiar brand degerminated variety. (You will have noticeably better tasting and better looking results). Because of its shorter shelf life, however, you will want to store your stone-ground cornmeal in the refrigerator or freezer.*

**1 cup stone-ground yellow cornmeal**
**1 cup all-purpose flour**
**2 teaspoons baking powder**
**1/2 teaspoon kosher salt**
**1/2 teaspoon baking soda**
**2 large eggs**
**2/3 cup milk**
**2/3 cup low fat buttermilk**
**1 tablespoon granulated sugar**
**2 tablespoons butter, melted**

Preheat the oven to 425 degrees. Grease a 9 x 9-inch baking pan; set aside.

Whisk the cornmeal, flour, baking powder, salt, and baking soda together in a large bowl; set aside. In a separate bowl, beat the eggs slightly. Add milk, buttermilk, sugar, and melted butter; whisk well. With a spoon or spatula, stir the egg mixture into the cornmeal mixture until just combined. Don't worry if you still have a few lumps; just don't over-mix.

Pour batter into prepared pan. Bake for 20-25 minutes until the top is golden brown and has pulled away slightly from the edges of the pan. Cut into squares; serve warm with butter and honey.

# Cherry Bread

*Makes 1 loaf*

*This special bread is a pretty holiday favorite. Because whole cherries are used, they are sliced when the bread is sliced.*

1 cup granulated sugar
1 1/2 cups all-purpose flour
1/2 teaspoon baking powder
1/2 teaspoon kosher salt
2 eggs, well-beaten
1/2 cup chopped nuts (optional)
1 (8-ounce) bottle of cherries with juice

Preheat oven to 350 degrees. Generously grease a 9 x 5 x 3-inch loaf pan; set aside.

Whisk the sugar, flour, baking powder, and salt together in a medium bowl. Drain the cherries, reserving the juice. Add the eggs and reserved cherry juice to the flour mixture; mix well. Fold the cherries (keep them whole) and nuts into batter. Spoon into prepared pan.

Bake 45 minutes until top springs back when lightly touched. Cool thoroughly on a wire rack before slicing to serve.

COOKING with CONFIDENCE

# Cranberry Bread

*Makes 1 loaf*

*With small cranberry-tart bursts of flavor, this bread is a special brunch or coffee break treat.*

1 cup granulated sugar
2 tablespoons shortening, melted
1 egg
2 cups all-purpose flour
1 1/2 teaspoons baking powder
1/2 teaspoon baking soda
1/2 teaspoon kosher salt
2 tablespoons hot water
1/2 cup orange juice
1 1/2 tablespoons grated orange rind
1 cup fresh cranberries, halved
1/2 cup walnuts, chopped

Preheat oven to 350 degrees. Grease and flour a 9 x 5 x 3-inch loaf pan; set aside.

In a large bowl, combine sugar and shortening; mix to a creamy consistency. Add egg; beat well. In a separate bowl, combine flour, baking powder, soda, and salt. Fold half of the flour mixture into the egg mixture, followed by half of the hot water and orange juice. Repeat the process, using remaining flour mixture and liquid. Fold in orange rind, cranberries, and walnuts.

Spoon batter in prepared pan. Bake 1 hour or until top springs back when lightly touched, and sides pull slightly away from the edges of the pan.

Cool thoroughly on a wire rack before slicing to serve.

# Easy Banana Bread

*Makes 1 loaf*

*Using very ripe bananas is key for obtaining the deepest banana flavor and nicest texture.*

1 3/4 cup mashed bananas (about 3 large)
1 cup granulated sugar
1 egg, beaten
1 1/2 cups all-purpose flour
1 teaspoon baking soda
3/4 teaspoon kosher salt
2 tablespoons butter, melted

Preheat oven to 325 degrees. Grease a 9 x 5 x 3-inch loaf pan; set aside.

Measure mashed bananas into a medium bowl. Add sugar and beaten egg; mix well. In a separate bowl, combine flour, soda, and salt. Stir the flour mixture into the banana mixture. Mix in melted butter.

Spoon batter into prepared pan. Bake 1 hour, 5 minutes or until a toothpick inserted in the center of the loaf comes out clean. Let rest 5 minutes in the pan; turn out onto a wire rack to cool.

COOKING WITH CONFIDENCE

# Lemon Tea Bread

*A tangy, fresh-tasting bread that's easy to make.*

**3/4 cup butter, softened**
**1 cup granulated sugar**
**1 1/2 teaspoons fresh lemon peel, finely shredded**
**3 eggs, beaten**
**2 1/4 cups all-purpose flour**
**1/4 teaspoon kosher salt**
**1/2 teaspoon baking soda**
**3/4 cup buttermilk**

*Glaze:*
**3 tablespoons fresh lemon juice**
**3/4 cup confectioners' sugar**

Preheat oven to 350 degrees. Grease a 9 x 5 x 3-inch loaf pan; set aside.

In a large mixing bowl, combine butter, sugar, and lemon peel; beat until light and creamy. Add eggs; mix well.

In a separate bowl, combine flour, salt, and soda; whisk to blend well. Add about half of the flour mixture and then half of the buttermilk to the egg mixture; stir well. Repeat procedure with remaining flour and buttermilk.

Spoon batter into prepared pan. Bake 55-60 minutes or until a wooden pick inserted in the center of the loaf comes out clean. Note: It will sink a little in the center and be doughy if it's not totally done. If you're not sure, allow a little more baking time to be on the safe side. Allow to rest in the pan for 5 minutes and then turn out onto a wire rack.

For the glaze, stir confectioners' sugar and lemon juice together until sugar is dissolved. Tip the loaf right side up on the wire rack. Using a toothpick or similar tool, pierce the top of the loaf several times. Spoon the glaze over the entire top. Allow bread to cool completely before slicing.

# Pumpkin Bread

*Makes 2 loaves*

*You will appreciate the ease of turning out two perfect loaves of this most-popular bread. Excellent served with flavored butter, cream cheese, or a good cheddar.*

2/3 cup vegetable shortening
2 cups granulated sugar
4 eggs
1 (15-ounce) can pumpkin
3 1/2 cups all-purpose flour
1 teaspoon baking powder
2 teaspoons baking soda
2 teaspoons cinnamon
1/2 teaspoon kosher salt
1/2 teaspoon cloves
1/2 teaspoon nutmeg

Preheat oven to 350 degrees. Generously grease two 9 x 5 x 3-inch loaf pans; set aside.

In a large mixing bowl, combine shortening and sugar; mix until light and creamy. In a medium bowl, beat eggs until thick and frothy; add pumpkin and mix well. Combine the pumpkin mixture with the sugar mixture, beating very slowly to blend. In a separate bowl, whisk flour, baking powder, soda, cinnamon, salt, cloves, and nutmeg together; add gradually to the pumpkin mixture. Because the batter is very thick, double check to make sure all ingredients are well blended.

Divide the batter evenly between the two prepared pans. Bake 1 hour, or until a wooden toothpick inserted in the center of the loaf comes out clean. Allow to rest in pans for 5 minutes; turn out onto a wire rack to cool.

Serve warm or at room temperature. Freezes well.

# Rhubarb Quick Bread

*Makes 2 loaves*

*Either fresh or frozen rhubarb can be used; however, using fresh from the garden gives you optimum results. If you're using frozen, sliced supermarket rhubarb, cut the pieces smaller than they come in the package, and make sure any ice crystals are removed before adding the pieces to your batter.*

## Bread:
1 1/2 cups brown sugar
2/3 cup vegetable oil
1 egg
1 teaspoon pure vanilla extract
1 1/2 cups fresh (or frozen) rhubarb, diced small
1/2 cup walnuts, chopped
1 cup low fat buttermilk
2 1/2 cups all-purpose flour
1 teaspoon kosher salt
1 teaspoon baking soda

## Topping:
1/2 cup granulated sugar
1 tablespoon butter, softened

Preheat oven to 325 degrees. Grease and flour two 9 x 5 x 3-inch loaf pans; set aside.

In medium bowl, mix brown sugar and oil. Add egg and vanilla; beat well. Fold in rhubarb and walnuts. In a separate bowl, whisk flour, salt, and soda together. Add buttermilk and the flour mixture alternately to the rhubarb mixture, stirring until well mixed. Divide batter evenly between the prepared pans.

For topping, combine sugar and butter; sprinkle on top of batters.

Bake 60-70 minutes until toothpick inserted in the center of the loaf comes out clean. Remove from oven and let rest in pans for 5 minutes; turn out onto a wire rack to cool completely before slicing.

# Apple Pecan Muffins

*Makes 18*

*These have a nice, brown sugary taste --- perfect with a cold summer salad.*

**1 cup light brown sugar, packed**
**1/2 cup dark brown sugar, packed**
**2/3 cup oil**
**1 egg**
**1 teaspoon pure vanilla extract**
**2 1/2 cups all-purpose flour**
**1 teaspoon baking soda**
**1 teaspoon kosher salt**
**1/2 teaspoon cinnamon**
**1/4 teaspoon nutmeg**
**1/4 teaspoon cloves**
**1 cup buttermilk**
**2 cups apples - peeled, cored, and finely diced**
**1/2 cup chopped pecans**

Preheat oven to 350 degrees. Generously grease muffin pans; set aside.

Combine brown sugars, oil, egg, and vanilla in a large bowl; beat well. In a separate bowl, mix flour, soda, salt, cinnamon, nutmeg, and cloves. Add 1/2 of the flour mixture and 1/2 of the buttermilk to the egg mixture; stir well. Repeat procedure with remaining flour and buttermilk; stir until no visible traces of flour remain. Fold in apples and pecans.

Spoon batter into prepared pans, filling cups 2/3 full. Bake 15-20 minutes or until top springs back when lightly touched. Loosen edges with a knife; turn out onto a wire rack to cool.

COOKING with CONFIDENCE

# Banana Chocolate Chip Muffins

*Makes 18*

*Oh, so close to being dessert. An interesting flavor combination.*

1 cup brown sugar, packed
1/4 cup butter, softened
2 eggs, slightly beaten
1/2 cup buttermilk
1 teaspoon pure vanilla extract
2 cups mashed bananas (about 4 large)
1 cup semisweet chocolate chips
3/4 cup chopped walnuts
2 cups all-purpose flour
1/2 teaspoon kosher salt
1/2 teaspoon baking powder
1/2 teaspoon baking soda

Preheat oven to 350 degrees. Coat muffin tins generously with non-stick vegetable spray; set aside.

In large mixing bowl, combine sugar and butter until creamy. Add eggs, buttermilk, vanilla, bananas, chocolate chips, and walnuts; stir until blended. In a separate bowl, stir flour, salt, baking powder and soda together. Add flour mixture to the banana mixture; stir just until no visible traces of flour remain. (Batter will be very thick). Spoon into prepared pans, filling muffin cups 3/4 full.

Bake 20-25 minutes until edges of muffins are golden brown and the tops spring back when lightly touched. Turn out onto a wire rack to cool.

# Corn Muffins

*These are delicious served with soup or salad.*

1 cup all-purpose flour
1 cup stone-ground cornmeal
2 tablespoons granulated sugar
1 1/2 teaspoons baking powder
1/4 teaspoon baking soda
1/4 teaspoon kosher salt
2 tablespoons cold butter
3/4 cup canned cream-style corn
2/3 cup buttermilk
1 egg, slightly beaten
1/2 cup oil-packed, sun-dried tomatoes (drained and diced)

Preheat oven to 425 degrees. Generously grease muffin pan; set aside.

Combine flour, cornmeal, sugar, baking powder, soda, and salt in a large mixing bowl; stir well. Cut butter in small pieces and add to the flour mixture; mix with a pastry blender or fork until crumbly. In a separate bowl, combine corn, buttermilk, and egg. Add corn mixture to flour mixture, stirring until no visible traces of flour remain.

Spoon batter into prepared pan. Bake 18-20 minutes until golden brown and firm to the touch. Serve warm.

COOKING WITH CONFIDENCE

# French Apple Muffins

*Delicate taste and texture, similar to a French doughnut. These are best served warm.*

## Muffins:
1/4 cup butter, softened
1/2 cup granulated sugar
1 egg, well beaten
1 cup milk
2 cups all-purpose flour
3 1/2 teaspoons baking powder
1/2 teaspoon cinnamon
1/4 teaspoon nutmeg
1 1/2 cups apples - peeled, cored, and finely diced

## Topping:
3 tablespoons confectioners' sugar
1/4 teaspoon cinnamon
2 tablespoons butter, melted

Preheat oven to 400 degrees. Coat muffin tins liberally with non-stick vegetable spray; set aside.

In a medium bowl, beat softened butter and sugar until creamy; stir in egg until well combined. In a separate bowl, whisk flour, baking powder, cinnamon, and nutmeg together. Add about half of the milk and half of the flour mixture to the egg mixture; stir well. Repeat with remaining milk and flour mixtures. Fold in chopped apples. Spoon into prepared pans.

For topping, mix confectioners' sugar and cinnamon; sprinkle about 1/2 teaspoon of the mixture over each of the muffins. Bake 15 minutes or until tops are firm to the touch. Remove pan from the oven. Drizzle about 1/2 teaspoon of the melted butter over each; sprinkle once again with confectioners' sugar mixture. Return the pan to the oven to bake additional 2 minutes. Use a knife to loosen edges; transfer to a wire rack. Serve warm if possible.

# Morning Glory Muffins

*Makes 20*

*Preparing a day in advance of serving will allow flavors to mellow and blend.*

3 eggs, beaten
1 cup vegetable oil
2 teaspoons pure vanilla extract
1 (8-ounce) can crushed pineapple, drained
1 1/2 cups grated carrots
1 cup grated apples (about 2 medium)
1/2 cup raisins
1/2 cup shredded coconut
1/2 cup pecans, finely chopped
1 1/4 cups granulated sugar
1/2 cup brown sugar, packed
2 1/4 cups all-purpose flour
2 teaspoons baking soda
2 teaspoons cinnamon
1/2 teaspoon nutmeg
1/4 teaspoon cloves
1/2 teaspoon kosher salt

Preheat oven to 375 degrees. Coat muffin tins liberally with non-stick vegetable spray; set aside.

In a large bowl, mix beaten eggs, oil, vanilla, and pineapple; stir in carrots, apples, raisins, coconut,pecans, and sugars. In a separate bowl, mix flour, soda, cinnamon, nutmeg, cloves, and salt. Add flour mixture to egg mixture; stir just until no visible traces of flour remain. Fill prepared muffin cups.

Bake 18-20 minutes or until top springs back when lightly touched. Turn out onto a wire rack to cool.

COOKING WITH CONFIDENCE

# Orange Muffins

*An all-purpose, flavorful muffin for coffee-time or brunch.*

## Muffins:
1/2 cup butter, softened
1/2 cup vegetable shortening
1 cup granulated sugar
2 eggs
1 teaspoon baking soda
1 cup buttermilk
2 cups all-purpose flour
1 1/2 tablespoons grated orange rind

## Topping:
2 tablespoons frozen orange juice concentrate, thawed
1/3 cup brown sugar, packed

Preheat oven to 400 degrees. Coat muffin pans with non-stick vegetable spray; set aside.

For the muffins, combine butter, shortening, and sugar in a medium mixing bowl. Add eggs; beat until creamy and light. Dissolve soda in buttermilk; add alternately with the flour to the egg mixture. Mix gently until no visible traces of flour remain. Stir in orange rind.

Fill muffin cups 2/3 full; bake 10 minutes. Turn oven temperature to Off, leaving the pans in the oven for additional 5-8 minutes until tops of the muffins spring back when lightly touched.

For the topping, dissolve brown sugar in orange concentrate. Remove muffins from the oven. Spoon a small amount of the topping over the warm muffins while still in the pan. Transfer to a wire rack to cool.

# Strawberry Muffins

*Makes 15*

*Minimum effort, maximum taste.*

## Muffins:
1/2 cup butter, softened
1 cup granulated sugar
2 eggs
1 teaspoon pure vanilla extract
2 cups all-purpose flour
2 teaspoons baking powder
1/4 teaspoon kosher salt
1/2 cup heavy cream
1 1/2 cups fresh strawberries*, hulled and finely chopped
*or substitute frozen strawberries - thawed, chopped, and very well drained

## Topping:
1 1/2 tablespoons granulated sugar

Preheat oven to 375 degrees. Generously coat muffin tins with non-stick vegetable spray; set aside.

In a large mixing bowl, beat softened butter and sugar until creamy. Add eggs one at a time, beating after each addition, until mixture is pale yellow. Stir in vanilla. In a separate bowl, combine flour, baking powder, and salt. Gently stir in half of the flour mixture and then half of the milk. Repeat the process with remaining flour and milk. Fold in strawberries.

Spoon into muffin cups, dividing equally and filling nearly to the top. Sprinkle each muffin with about 1/4 teaspoon sugar. Bake 20-25 minutes or until top springs back when lightly touched. Let rest in pan for about 2-3 minutes; loosen edges with a knife and turn out onto a wire rack to cool.

# Triple Chocolate Muffins

*Makes 12*

*For the chocolate lover in the house. Can be served warm or cold.*

## Muffins:
4 (1-ounce) squares unsweetened chocolate
1/4 cup butter
2 eggs
2/3 cup granulated sugar
3/4 cup milk
1 1/2 cups all-purpose flour
1/4 cup unsweetened cocoa powder
2 teaspoons baking powder
1 teaspoon baking soda
1 cup semisweet chocolate chips
1/2 cup walnuts, chopped

## Topping:
1/3 cup granulated sugar
2 tablespoons unsweetened cocoa powder
1/4 cup all-purpose flour
2 tablespoons butter, melted

Preheat oven to 350 degrees. Coat muffin tins liberally with non-stick vegetable spray; set aside. Combine chocolate and butter in a small saucepan. Stir over very low heat until chocolate has melted; set aside to cool.

For the topping, combine sugar, cocoa, flour, and melted butter in a small bowl; mix well and set aside.

For the muffins, beat eggs in a medium bowl until frothy. Add sugar, milk, and cooled chocolate mixture; stir until well mixed. In a separate bowl, whisk flour, cocoa, baking powder, and soda together. Fold flour mixture into the egg mixture; stir until no visible traces of flour remain. The batter will be very thick. Fold in chips and walnuts.

Spoon into prepared pan, filling the cups 3/4 full. Sprinkle about a tablespoon of topping on each muffin; pat topping down gently. Bake 16-18 minutes or until top springs back when lightly touched. Turn out onto a wire rack for cooling.

# Scoops of Confidence

## For Breakfast, Brunches and Breads

**Egg whites** are high in protein and low in fat. They whip the best when warm. **Egg yolks** contain the taste, but they are high in fat. Egg whites and yolks are easier to separate when eggs are cold. **Store your eggs** with the narrow end facing down in the carton to keep the yolks centered.

**Chicken/egg trivia**, aka more than you needed to know: The color of a hen's ear lobes, located behind her eyes, will tell you if eggs will be brown or white. White lobes indicate white eggs; red lobes indicate brown or tinted eggs.

Need a quick **breakfast on the go** - try a **breakfast wrap.** Use a good quality, large (burrito size) flour tortilla as your base. Warm it gently for greater "wrapability". Select your choice of filling (scrambled eggs and ham, cream cheese and strawberries - whatever is in the refrigerator). Center the filling, fold up the bottom, fold in the sides, and you're on your way.

Make your own **compound butters** to have on hand for muffins, scones, or toast. You will want to start with room temperature butter; add various ingredients (complementing your food) to create intensity and depth. Mixing by hand takes only a few seconds. If you're not using the butter immediately, form a small 1 1/2-inch roll on waxed paper (for easy slicing), transfer to a heavy duty plastic bag, label, and freeze. Here are a few **compound butter ideas:**

**Orange:** 1/2 cup butter, 1 tablespoon each of frozen orange juice concentrate and rind

**Strawberry:** 1/2 cup butter, 1pint strawberries (mashed), 3/4 cup confectioners' sugar

**Apricot:** 1/2 cup butter, 1/4 cup cooked dried apricots, 2 teaspoons granulated sugar, 2 teaspoons grated orange rind

**Cranberry:** 3/4 cup butter, 1 cup fresh cranberries (finely chopped) 2 teaspoons granulated sugar, and 2 teaspoons grated orange rind

**Herb:** 1/2 cup butter, 1/2 teaspoon dried rosemary (crushed), 1/2 teaspoon dried thyme, just a pinch of each dried sage and basil

**Applesauce** may be substituted in equal amounts for oil in **quick bread** and **muffin** recipes.

*Petroselinum crispum*

(Parsley)

# Soups and Salads

Chicken 'n Dumplings Soup
Chicken Wild Rice Soup
Clam Chowder
Corn Chowder
Herbed Tomato Soup
Italian Mushroom Soup
Seven Can Chili
B L T Salad
Bacon Parmesan Salad
Cabbage and Apple Slaw
Chicken Wild Rice Salad
French Potato Salad
Frozen Cranberry Salad
Grasshopper Salad
Fruit and Cream Salad
Greens with Fruit and Cheese
Ham Salad for 25
Marinated Broccoli Salad
Orange Coleslaw
Pear and Blue Cheese Salad
Shrimp Pasta Salad
Superb Spinach Salad
Sweet Broccoli Salad
Terrific Black Bean Salad
Tomato-Mushroom Platter
Year 'Round Garden Salad
Blue Cheese Dressing
Dill Ranch Dressing
Easy French Dressing
Fresh Lemon Vinaigrette
Fresh Raspberry Vinaigrette
Orange Dijon Dressing
Poppyseed Dressing
Raspberry Dressing

Scoops of Confidence

# Chicken 'n Dumplings Soup

*8 servings*

*We all like chicken soup. But starting with a chicken instead of a can? There's absolutely nothing like it. Use your creative license to add whatever vegetables and seasonings you like; this recipe is only the start.*

1 whole chicken, 3-4 pounds
1 large onion, chopped
3 large stalks of celery, chopped
2 bay leaves
8-9 cups water
Kosher salt
Freshly ground black pepper
3 cups carrots, sliced
8 ounces mushrooms, sliced
1 1/2 cups fresh or frozen peas

*Great Dumplings:*
1 egg
1/4 cup milk
1/4 cup half and half
1 1/2 cups all-purpose flour
2 teaspoons baking powder
1/2 teaspoon kosher salt
1 tablespoon fresh herbs of your choice (or 1 teaspoon dried)

Wash the chicken; cut into large pieces of uniform size. Place the chicken pieces, onions, celery, and bay leaves in a large pot. Add enough water to cover the chicken pieces by at least 2 inches; bring to a boil. Using a large spoon, skim off any foam; discard. Add salt and pepper to taste. Simmer chicken for about 45 minutes or until tender. Transfer cooked chicken from the pot to a colander to drain and cool. Discard bay leaves. Add carrots and mushrooms; cook 8 minutes. When the chicken is cool, remove skin and discard. Pull meat from the bones. Toss chicken pieces with salt and pepper to taste; set aside.

For the dumplings, beat the egg slightly in a medium bowl. Add milk and half and half; mix well. Stirring with a fork, add flour, baking powder, salt, and herbs to form a very thick batter. Drop by teaspoonful into the soup. Note: Dumplings grow and plump up to twice their size, so give them adequate room. Cover the pot and simmer on low heat for 15 minutes. Do not lift the cover during this time (trust me, this works). At the end of the 15 minutes, remove the cover; add the peas and seasoned chicken pieces. Bring soup back to a simmer and serve.

# Chicken Wild Rice Soup

*6 servings*

*A hearty soup that you'll want to make again and again.*

4 strips bacon, diced
2/3 cup uncooked wild rice, rinsed thoroughly
1/2 cup onions, chopped
1/2 cup carrots, diced small
1/2 cup celery, diced small
1 cup fresh mushrooms, sliced
2 cloves garlic, minced
4 cups low-sodium chicken broth
1 1/2 cups cooked chicken, cut in 1/2-inch cubes
1 1/2 cups heavy cream
2 tablespoons butter
2 tablespoons flour
1/2 cup dry white wine
1/2 teaspoon kosher salt
1/4 teaspoon white pepper
2 tablespoons fresh chives, minced, for garnish

In a large, heavy pot or Dutch oven, cook and stir bacon until crisp; reserve about 2 tablespoons fat; remove bacon from the pan. Cook and stir rice, onion, carrots, and celery in the reserved fat for 4 minutes; add mushrooms and garlic; cook 1 additional minute.

Add chicken broth and bacon. Heat to boiling, stirring constantly. Reduce heat. Cover and simmer, stirring occasionally, about 40 minutes or until rice is tender. Stir in chicken and cream. Mix butter and flour; whisk into the soup. Cook and stir about 2 minutes until soup has thickened. Add wine, salt, and pepper. Reheat slowly; do not boil. Spoon into bowls; garnish with fresh chives.

COOKING WITH CONFIDENCE

# Clam Chowder

*One of the loveliest of cold weather treats.*

**2 cups red potatoes, diced (do not peel)**
**1 1/2 cups water**
**1 (8-ounce) bottle clam juice, divided**
**6 slices bacon, diced**
**3 tablespoons butter**
**1/2 cup onions, diced**
**1/2 cup celery, diced**
**1 tablespoon minced garlic**
**1/2 cup all-purpose flour**
**2 (6 1/2-ounce) cans chopped clams, undrained**
**1/2 teaspoon dried thyme**
**1/2 teaspoon celery salt**
**1/8 teaspoon freshly ground black pepper**
**3/4 cup milk**
**3/4 cup heavy cream**
**2 tablespoons fresh parsley for garnish**

Combine diced potatoes, water and 1/2 cup clam juice in a saucepan; cook 10 minutes. Do not drain.

Cook bacon in a small skillet until brown and crispy; remove and set aside. Add butter to the skillet. Stir in onions and celery; cook 2 minutes. Add garlic and flour; cook and stir 3 minutes.

Combine cooked potato mixture, bacon, onion mixture, clams, thyme, celery salt, pepper, milk, and cream in a large saucepan. Simmer over low heat for 8-10 minutes. Serve hot; garnish with parsley.

# Corn Chowder

*6 servings*

*Such a good tasting, hearty soup that can be on the table in less than 30 minutes.*

**6 slices thick bacon, diced**
**1 cup onions, chopped**
**1/2 cup celery, diced**
**1 large clove garlic, minced**
**2 cups red potatoes, diced**
**1 (15-ounce) can creamed corn**
**1 (15-ounce) can whole kernel corn***
**3 cups milk**
**1/2 teaspoon kosher salt**
**1/4 teaspoon freshly ground black pepper**

<u>*Garnish:*</u>
**1 tablespoon fresh parsley (or 1 teaspoon dried)**
**1 tablespoon fresh chives (or 1 teaspoon dried)**

\*      2 cups fresh corn, cut from the cob, may be substituted. Add 1 teaspoon granulated sugar, and increase amount of salt if desired. Taste before adjusting the seasonings.

Cook and stir bacon pieces in a Dutch oven or large skillet over medium heat until crisp and brown. Add onion, celery, garlic, and potatoes; cook and stir for 10-12 minutes until potatoes are crisp-tender. Add corn, milk, salt, and pepper; simmer (do not boil) for 10 minutes.

To serve, ladle hot soup into bowls. Garnish with parsley and chives.

COOKING WITH CONFIDENCE

# Herbed Tomato Soup

*6 servings*

*A flavorful twist on classic tomato soup.*

**3 tablespoons butter**
**1 cup yellow onions, diced**
**2 (15-ounce) cans diced tomatoes**
**1 tablespoon dried basil**
**1/2 teaspoon dried thyme**
**3/4 teaspoon dried oregano**
**1 tablespoon granulated garlic**
**1/2 teaspoon kosher salt**
**1/2 teaspoon white pepper**
**2 (15-ounce) cans low sodium chicken broth**
**2 cups half and half**
**1 cup heavy cream**
**4 tablespoons butter**
**1/3 cup all-purpose flour**
**2 fresh tomatoes, seeded and diced**
**1 clove garlic, minced**
**2 teaspoons dill weed**

*Garnish:*
**Freshly grated Parmesan cheese**

Melt butter in a heavy Dutch oven or large skillet. Add onions; cook and stir over medium heat for 6-8 minutes or until onions are tender. Add canned tomatoes, basil, thyme, oregano, garlic, salt, pepper, and chicken broth; simmer 15 minutes, stirring occasionally. In a small saucepan, warm half and half and heavy cream; whisk into tomato mixture to blend well.

Melt butter in heavy stockpot; add flour and stir constantly over medium heat for 3-4 minutes. Slowly add tomato and cream mixture; whisk to blend well. Add fresh tomatoes, garlic, and dill weed; simmer gently for additional 3 minutes. Ladle hot soup into bowls; garnish with grated Parmesan cheese.

# Italian Mushroom Soup

*Served with a warm and crusty Italian bread, this soup is perfect for a hearty winter lunch.*

2 tablespoons butter
1 cup onions, finely chopped
2 cups sliced mushrooms
2 cloves garlic, minced
3 cups chicken broth
1 (3-ounce) can tomato paste
1/2 cup dry white wine
3 egg yolks
1/2 cup Parmesan cheese
2 tablespoons dried parsley
1/2 teaspoon dried oregano
1/2 teaspoon dried basil
1/2 teaspoon dried rosemary, finely ground
1/4 teaspoon dried sage
1/4 teaspoon dried marjoram

Melt butter in large Dutch oven. Add onions and mushrooms; stir and cook for 5 minutes. Add garlic; cook additional minute. Stir in chicken broth, tomato paste and wine; blend well. Simmer for 3 minutes.

Make a thickening paste by combining egg yolks, Parmesan cheese, parsley, oregano, basil, rosemary, sage and marjoram in a bowl. Add about 2 cups of the hot broth to thin the paste; stir well. Whisk entire mixture into the remaining hot broth.

Bring the soup back to a simmer; do not boil. Serve immediately.

# Seven Can Chili

*As you may have guessed, there are 7 cans of stuff in this version. And you must know there are no hard and fast rules when it comes to making chili. Some like it hot, some do not. So try this milder version first, and hike up the spices if you wish. I like the combination of kidney and black beans for both taste and texture.*

1/4 cup canola oil
1 1/4 cups onions, diced
1 cup celery, diced
3/4 cup carrots, diced
3 cloves fresh garlic, minced
2 pounds lean ground beef
1 teaspoon kosher salt
1/2 teaspoon freshly ground black pepper
1 1/2 tablespoons medium hot chili powder
1/2 teaspoon cumin
1 tablespoon paprika
1 tablespoon dried oregano
1/2 teaspoon dried red pepper flakes
2 (14-ounce) cans diced tomatoes
2 (8-ounce) cans tomato sauce
1 (6-ounce) can tomato paste
1 (15-ounce) can kidney beans, rinsed and drained
1 (15-ounce) can black beans, rinsed and drained
2 cups beef broth (or dark beer)

Heat oil in a large Dutch oven or heavy pan. Add onions, celery, and carrots; cook and stir until onions are soft and translucent (about 3 minutes). Stir in garlic; cook an additional minute. Add ground beef, salt, and pepper; break the beef into small chunks with a fork. Mix in chili powder, cumin, paprika, oregano, and red pepper; cook and stir over medium heat for about 8-10 minutes until the beef has turned brown.

Now you get to open all those cans - tomatoes, sauce, paste, kidney beans, black beans - and add the contents of each to the beef mixture. Stir in broth or beer. Cook at a low simmer for about 20 minutes; stir occasionally. Excellent served with shredded cheddar cheese, sour cream, and corn muffins.

# BLT Salad

*The same ingredients found in a BLT sandwich form a pretty, layered salad. If you have a trifle bowl with nice straight sides, this is a perfect time to use it.*

4 slices bacon
4 cups romaine or iceberg lettuce
1/2 cup mayonnaise
1 tablespoon finely chopped green onion
1 teaspoon white wine vinegar
1 teaspoon Dijon mustard
1 1/2 cups fresh tomatoes (about 2 large), seeded and finely diced
1/4 teaspoon kosher salt
1/8 teaspoon freshly ground pepper
1 cup shredded mozzarella cheese
1/2 cup shredded cheddar cheese
1 cup black olives, sliced

Cut bacon into 1/4-inch pieces. In a medium skillet, cook and stir until crispy and brown; transfer to a paper towel to drain and cool.

To make salad, place half of the lettuce evenly in the bottom of a clear glass bowl. Combine mayonnaise, onion, vinegar, and mustard; spread half of this mixture in a thin layer over the lettuce. Mix diced tomatoes with salt and pepper; spoon half of the amount over the mayonnaise layer. Mix the two cheeses; sprinkle half of the mixture over the tomatoes, followed by half of the bacon pieces and half of the olives.

Repeat procedure with remaining ingredients.

Cover bowl tightly with plastic wrap; refrigerate for 1-2 hours before serving.

# Bacon Parmesan Salad

*8 servings*

*This is a terrific salad for those who love texture and crunch, and particularly wonderful for those who aren't even sure they like cauliflower.*

<u>Salad:</u>
**2 hearts of romaine and 1/2 head iceberg lettuce***
**2 cups cauliflower florets, minced**
**1 pound lean bacon, cut into 1/2-inch pieces**
**1 cup freshly ground Parmesan cheese**

<u>Dressing:</u>
**1 cup mayonnaise**
**2 tablespoons white wine vinegar**
**1/3 cup granulated sugar**
**3 tablespoons milk**

For salad, cut core from romaine; cut in half lengthwise, then thinly slice to ribbons. Core, then cut iceberg lettuce into uniformly sized pieces. Use a food processor or chop cauliflower by hand into extra tiny pieces. Using a large skillet, cook and stir bacon pieces over medium heat until crisp and brown; transfer to a paper towel to drain and cool.

For dressing, whisk mayonnaise, vinegar, sugar, and milk together in a small bowl.

To assemble salad, combine lettuces, cauliflower, bacon, and cheese in a large bowl. Add dressing; toss to mix thoroughly.

*        May substitute 1 (16-ounce) package iceberg salad mix

# Cabbage and Apple Slaw

*This coleslaw has a crisp, distinctive taste. It is also very tasty as an extra layer in sandwiches or burgers, serving as both the green and the crunch.*

## Salad:
3 cups shredded cabbage
2 cups apples, cored and julienned
1 cup dried cranberries or raisins
3/4 cup diced celery
1/4 cup diced onion

## Dressing:
2/3 cup mayonnaise
2 tablespoons lemon juice
2 tablespoons Dijon mustard
1 teaspoon celery seed
1 teaspoon dried dill weed
1/4 teaspoon kosher salt
1/8 teaspoon freshly ground pepper

In a large bowl, combine cabbage, apples, cranberries or raisins, celery, and onions.

For the dressing, whisk mayonnaise, lemon juice, mustard, celery seed, dill, salt, and pepper together until creamy and well blended. Toss the dressing with the cabbage mixture.

Cover and refrigerate at least 2 hours to blend flavors.

# Chicken Wild Rice Salad

*6-8 servings*

*A hearty, do-ahead salad with a garlic-mustard dressing to give it some spirit.*

## Salad:
1 cup uncooked wild rice
6 cups chicken broth (canned or homemade)
1 cup toasted pecans*
2 tablespoons fresh lemon juice
1 chicken breast, cooked, cooled, and cut into bite-size pieces
4 green onions, sliced
3/4 cup diced red bell pepper
1 cup fresh sugar snap peas, cut in 1/2-inch pieces
2 avocados, diced

## Dressing:
1/3 cup vegetable oil
1/4 cup rice vinegar
4 cloves garlic, minced
1 tablespoon Dijon mustard
1/2 teaspoon kosher salt
1/4 teaspoon freshly ground black pepper

Wash wild rice thoroughly in cold water; drain. Transfer rice to a large saucepan. Add cold water to cover, and cook 15 minutes; drain. Add chicken broth. Cover;  cook gently for about 25 minutes, stirring occasionally, until rice is tender and most of the kernels have popped open. Stir in lemon juice; set aside

\*        To toast pecans, preheat oven to 350 degrees. Place pecans in a shallow pan and bake, stirring occasionally, for 8-10 minutes or until golden brown. Remove from oven; set aside to cool.

For the dressing, whisk oil, vinegar, garlic, mustard, salt, and pepper together; set aside.

To assemble salad, combine chicken pieces, onions, red pepper, and peas; add to cooled wild rice. Add avocados and toasted pecans; stir gently to blend well. Add dressing to salad; stir gently but thoroughly. Cover; refrigerate at least 3 hours, allowing dressing to absorb and flavors to blend. Serve cold.

# French Potato Salad

*6 servings*

*Inspired by a side dish enjoyed in the Alsace region of northeastern France, this is a nice alternative to the usual mayonnaise-based version. Try it with a hot grilled bratwurst and a little mustard on the side.*

2 1/2 pounds small, red potatoes
1 1/2 cups celery, sliced
3/4 cup fresh parsley, chopped
1 1/2 red (or green) bell pepper, diced
1 pound lean bacon
3 tablespoons bacon drippings
1 bunch green onions, thinly sliced
1 clove fresh garlic, minced
3/4 cup cider vinegar
1/4 cup granulated sugar
3/4 teaspoon freshly ground black pepper
3/4 teaspoon caraway seed
3/4 teaspoon dried dill weed
2 cups cherry tomatoes for garnish

Starting with cold water to cover and about 1 1/2 teaspoons salt, cook potatoes in a partially covered pan until tender but still firm. Drain cooked potatoes; allow to cool. Peel and slice potatoes into uniform-sized pieces. Combine sliced potatoes with celery, parsley, and peppers in a large bowl; set aside.

Cook bacon in a skillet until crisp; transfer to paper towels to drain. Cook onions in the reserved fat until translucent. Add garlic; cook an additional minute. Combine vinegar, sugar, pepper, caraway, and dill; add to the onions and garlic in the skillet. Bring to a simmer over medium heat.

Crumble the bacon and add to the potato mixture. Pour hot mixture from the skillet over the potatoes and toss lightly to coat. Garnish with cherry tomatoes; serve warm or at room temperature.

COOKING WITH CONFIDENCE

# Frozen Cranberry Salad

*6-8 servings*

*A nice, mild cranberry salad, especially delicious with turkey or pheasant.*

**2 (3-ounce) packages cream cheese, softened**
**3 tablespoons confectioners' sugar**
**2 tablespoons mayonnaise or salad dressing**
**1/2 cup walnuts, coarsely chopped**
**1 (16-ounce) can whole berry cranberry sauce**
**1 (8-ounce) can crushed pineapple, drained**
**1 cup heavy cream**

Combine cream cheese, sugar, and mayonnaise in a large bowl; beat until smooth. Stir in walnuts, cranberry sauce, and pineapple; mix well.

Beat cream until stiff peaks form; gently fold into cranberry mixture until well blended. Spoon into a shallow 11 x 7-inch pan. Cover with plastic wrap and freeze for several hours. Let stand at room temperature a few minutes before cutting into squares to serve.

# Grasshopper Salad

*6-8 servings*

*Whenever there's a family or community food event, my sister Kathie is expected to bring the green salad. Enough sugar to keep you hoppin' all day.*

**2 (3-ounce) packages lime gelatin**
**1 (3-ounce) package lemon gelatin**
**6 tablespoons granulated sugar**
**2 cups boiling water**
**1 cup cold water**
**1/3 cup white creme de cacao**
**1/3 cup green creme de menthe**
**1 tablespoon pure vanilla extract**
**1 cup heavy cream**

Dissolve lime gelatin, lemon gelatin, and sugar in the boiling water. Add cold water, creme de cacao, creme de menthe, and vanilla; stir to blend well. Refrigerate for 30 minutes or until thickened but not set. Coat a 6-cup ring mold with non-stick vegetable spray; set aside. Whip cream; fold into gelatin mixture. Spoon into prepared mold. Refrigerate until set. To serve, unmold salad onto a serving platter. May be garnished with candied spearmint leaves or maraschino cherries.

# Fruit and Cream Salad

*6 servings*

*Any kind of fruit (with the exception of melon) can be used in this salad. You are limited only by what's fresh at the market or canned in your pantry.*

## Salad:
2 cups fresh strawberries, quartered

1 cup green or red seedless grapes, halved

1 (11-ounce) can mandarin oranges, drained

1 (15-ounce) can sliced peaches, well drained (or 2 cups fresh peaches, sliced)

1 (8-ounce) can pineapple chunks, drained (reserve the syrup for dressing)

1 apple, peeled and diced

2 bananas, sliced

1 cup slivered almonds, toasted

## Dressing:
2/3 cup granulated sugar

2 tablespoons all-purpose flour

2 eggs, slightly beaten

2 tablespoons canola oil

1 cup pineapple juice

1/4 cup orange juice

3 tablespoons lemon juice (fresh or bottled)

1/2 cup heavy cream

For the dressing, mix sugar and flour in a medium saucepan. Add beaten eggs, oil, and juices. Cook over low heat, stirring constantly, until smooth and thick. Remove from heat; chill thoroughly. Beat cream until stiff peaks form. Gently fold cream into the chilled fruit dressing mixture.

To make the salad, combine strawberries, grapes, oranges, peaches, pineapple, and apple in a large bowl. Add the dressing a little at a time until fruit is coated. Just before serving, stir in bananas and almonds.

Leftover dressing can be covered and refrigerated for up to 5 days. (It's lovely as a side sauce with cake or bread pudding).

COOKING WITH CONFIDENCE

# Greens with Fruit and Cheese

*6 servings*

*Pretty as the picture, this salad is refreshing and light.*

## Salad:
4 cups mixed salad greens
1 1/2 cups fresh blueberries
3 kiwi fruit, peeled and sliced
2 apples, diced
2 red pears, sliced
1 1/2 cups fresh raspberries
1 cup walnuts
4 ounces goat cheese, crumbled

## Lemon Vinaigrette:
1/2 cup canola oil
1/4 cup fresh lemon juice
1 tablespoon fresh parsley, minced
1 teaspoon Dijon mustard
1 teaspoon fresh garlic, minced
1/2 teaspoon freshly grated lemon rind
3/4 teaspoon kosher salt
1/4 teaspoon freshly ground black pepper

For vinaigrette, grate rind from fresh lemon. Combine oil, juice, parsley, mustard, garlic, lemon rind, salt, and pepper in a small bowl; whisk well.

To make salad, combine greens, blueberries, kiwi fruit, apples, and pears in a large bowl; toss with vinaigrette. Sprinkle raspberries, walnuts, and crumbled cheese on top of the salad; serve with additional vinaigrette on the side. This salad also presents well in individual servings.

# Ham Salad for 25

*LARGE batch*

*When you need a recipe already "multiplied out" for a group, this is it. My brother Ellerd requests this whenever he and his family head for a family gathering. It's a do-the-night-before dish that serves as a popular staple.*

1 pound uncooked rotini
4-5 cups ham, cut in 1/2-inch cubes
3 cups celery, finely diced
1 cup onions, finely chopped
1 (4-ounce) jar pimentos, drained
9 hardboiled eggs, diced
3 cups mayonnaise or salad dressing
1 tablespoon kosher salt
1 tablespoon granulated sugar
2 teaspoons prepared mustard
1 (10-ounce) package frozen green peas, thawed
3 cups chopped cashews

Cook rotini according to directions on the package; drain and cool. In a large bowl, combine rotini, ham, celery, onions, pimentos and eggs; stir well. Cover the bowl and refrigerate overnight.

To finish salad, whisk mayonnaise, salt, sugar, and mustard together in a small bowl; pour over rotini and ham mixture. Add peas and cashews; stir thoroughly. Serve cold.

# Marinated Broccoli Salad

*6-8 servings*

*Here is a fool-proof, easy salad to make ahead of time. With only three main ingredients and a marinade, it's a quick one to put together.*

## Salad:
2 bunches broccoli (about 2 pounds)
1 pint cherry or grape tomatoes
2/3 cup black olives, drained and sliced

## Marinade:
3/4 cup canola oil
1/2 cup cider vinegar
1 clove garlic, minced
1 1/2 teaspoons dried dill weed
1/2 teaspoon granulated sugar
1/2 teaspoon kosher salt
1/2 teaspoon coarsely ground black pepper
1/4 teaspoon celery seed

Cut florets from broccoli. Peel remaining stalks; slice diagonally into 1/2-inch pieces. Add tomatoes and olives; transfer to a heavy duty zip top bag or a large glass bowl.

For marinade, whisk oil, vinegar, garlic, dill, sugar, salt, pepper, and celery seed together; pour over broccoli mixture. Remove as much air as possible from the bag before closing it or, if using a bowl, cover tightly with plastic wrap. Refrigerate for several hours to allow flavors to blend. Drain excess marinade from salad; transfer to a large bowl for serving.

# Orange Coleslaw

*A taste sensation varying from the old standard. I like to serve this with barbequed ribs.*

## Salad:
1/2 head (about 5 cups) finely shredded green cabbage
1/2 cup celery, finely diced
1 (4-ounce) can mandarin oranges, drained

## Dressing:
1/2 cup mayonnaise
1/2 cup heavy cream
4 tablespoons frozen orange juice concentrate, thawed
2 tablespoons rice vinegar
1/2 teaspoon dried dill weed
1/2 teaspoon celery seed
1/4 teaspoon kosher salt
1/8 teaspoon freshly ground black pepper

Mix shredded cabbage and celery in a large bowl.

For the dressing, whisk mayonnaise, cream, orange juice concentrate, vinegar, dill weed, celery seed, salt, and pepper in a small bowl until well blended. Add dressing to cabbage mixture; mix well. Cover; refrigerate at least 2 hours to allow flavors to blend. Gently stir in mandarin oranges just before serving.

# Pear and Blue Cheese Salad

*6-8 servings*

*Glazing the nuts with honey adds sweetness and crunch to the salad, and prevents the nuts from absorbing the dressing.*

## Salad:
8 cups mixed salad greens
2 fresh pears
2 tablespoons lemon juice

## Dressing:
1/3 cup canola oil
3 tablespoons raspberry vinegar
1 tablespoon chopped shallots
3/4 teaspoon granulated sugar
1/2 teaspoon kosher salt
1/8 teaspoon freshly ground black pepper

## Garnish:
4 ounces (about 1 cup) crumbled blue cheese
3/4 cup walnuts, glazed with 1 tablespoon honey

Glaze walnuts: Place 1 tablespoon honey in a small skillet. Add walnuts; cook and stir over low heat until nuts are slightly browned and completely glazed. Remove from heat and carefully (they are way hot!) transfer nuts to a glass plate to cool.

For dressing, combine oil, vinegar, shallots, sugar, salt, and pepper in a small bowl. Whisk to mix well.

To finish salad, dice (or slice) the pears; mix with lemon juice to prevent browning. Place salad greens on individual salad plates. Top with pears, glazed walnuts, and blue cheese crumbles. Drizzle with dressing.

As an alternate serving method, place salad greens in a large serving bowl with pears and walnuts. Add the dressing and toss lightly. Top with blue cheese crumbles; serve immediately.

# Superb Spinach Salad

*6-8 servings*

*So easy, so good.*

## Salad:
6 ounces baby spinach (about 8 cups)
3/4 cup macadamia nuts, coarsely chopped
3 kiwi fruit - peeled, halved, and sliced
1 1/2 cups fresh raspberries

## Dressing:
6 tablespoons raspberry vinegar
6 tablespoons raspberry preserves
1/3 cup canola oil

For the dressing, whisk vinegar, preserves, and oil together in a small bowl until well blended.

Lightly toss spinach with the dressing and approximately half of the nuts, kiwi fruit, and raspberries in a shallow salad bowl or on a platter. Top with remaining nuts, kiwi fruit, and raspberries.

Serve immediately.

NOTE: For a variation, replace the raspberry flavors with strawberries, strawberry vinegar, and strawberry preserves. Either version presents itself beautifully.

# Sweet Broccoli Salad

*6 servings*

*Here is a simple salad that will please everyone at the table, even those who are not ardent broccoli fans.*

<u>Salad:</u>
1/2 pound lean bacon, cut in small pieces
4 cups broccoli florets
1 1/2 cups celery, diced
1/2 cup green onions, sliced
1 1/2 cups seedless red or green grapes, halved
3/4 cup dried apricots, chopped finely (or 3/4 cup golden raisins)
2/3 cup slivered (or sliced) almonds

<u>Dressing:</u>
1 cup mayonnaise
2 tablespoon white wine vinegar
2 tablespoons granulated sugar

Using a skillet, cook and stir bacon pieces over medium heat until crisp and brown; transfer to a paper towel to drain and cool. In a large bowl, combine broccoli, celery, onions, grapes, and apricots.

Whisk mayonnaise, vinegar, and sugar together in a small bowl; add to broccoli mixture and mix well. Just before serving, stir in almonds.

# Terrific Black Bean Salad

*4 servings*

*Great to make in mid-summer using garden-fresh herbs.*

<u>Salad:</u>
2 (15-ounce) cans black beans, drained and rinsed
1 large tomato, diced
1 mango, peeled and diced
2 green onions, thinly sliced
2 tablespoons chopped red onion
1 tablespoon snipped fresh mint leaves
1 tablespoon snipped fresh cilantro

<u>Dressing:</u>
2 tablespoons mango flavored vinegar (or red wine vinegar)
2 tablespoons canola oil
2 teaspoons fresh lime juice
1/2 teaspoon minced garlic
1/4 teaspoon cayenne pepper
1/4 teaspoon kosher salt
1/8 teaspoon freshly ground black pepper

For the salad, combine beans and diced tomato in a medium bowl. Stir in diced mango, green and red onions, mint leaves and cilantro; mix well.

For the dressing, whisk vinegar and oil together in a small bowl. Add lime juice, minced garlic, cayenne pepper, salt, and pepper; mix well. Stir dressing into the salad.

Cover and refrigerate for several hours before serving, allowing flavors to blend.

COOKING WITH CONFIDENCE

# Tomato-Mushroom Platter

*6 servings*

*A wonderful summer side dish to make when fresh tomatoes are plentiful.*

**Salad:**
3 large slicing tomatoes
2 cups  fresh mushrooms, quartered

**Dressing:**
1/2 cup basil olive oil
2 tablespoons balsamic vinegar
2 tablespoons fresh basil, minced
1 tablespoon fresh parsley minced
1 clove garlic, minced
1 tablespoon finely chopped onion
1 teaspoon kosher salt
1 teaspoon dill weed
1/4 teaspoon freshly ground black pepper

**2 tablespoons green onions, finely sliced, for garnish**

Wash tomatoes and pat dry with a paper towel. Core, cut a very thin slice from the top and bottom of each tomato and discard. Cut remaining tomatoes into 1/2 inch slices; arrange slices in two rows on a shallow platter. Place mushrooms between the rows of tomatoes.

For the dressing, whisk oil, vinegar, basil, parsley, garlic, onion, salt, dill, and pepper together in a small bowl. Drizzle mixture over tomatoes and mushrooms. Sprinkle with green onions.

Cover with plastic wrap. Refrigerate 2-3 hours to allow flavors to meld. Serve cold.

# Year 'Round Garden Salad

*6-8 servings*

*Easy to make and serve in any season. Ingredients can be varied according to your taste and availability.*

<u>Salad:</u>
4 cups mixed salad greens
10-12 cherry tomatoes, halved
1 cup celery, finely diced
1 medium cucumber, seeded and diced
1 (10-ounce) package frozen green peas, thawed
1 cup carrots, cut in matchstick pieces (or thinly sliced)
1 cup cheddar cheese, shredded
2 tablespoons green onions, finely sliced

<u>Dressing:</u>
3/4 cup mayonnaise
1/2 cup sour cream
1 tablespoon lemon juice
1 teaspoon prepared mustard
2 teaspoons chopped parsley
1/2 teaspoon dried dill weed
1/4 teaspoon minced garlic
1/4 teaspoon kosher salt
1/8 teaspoon celery seed

Combine greens, tomatoes, celery, cucumber, peas, carrots, cheese, and onions in a large bowl.

For the dressing, combine mayonnaise, sour cream, lemon juice, and mustard in a small bowl; whisk until well blended. Stir in parsley, dill, garlic, salt, and celery seed.

Add dressing a little at a time to the mixed greens; toss. Cover and refrigerate any leftover dressing.

# Blue Cheese Dressing

*Makes about 1 1/2 cups*

*Use a good quality, crumbly cheese - with lots of "blue" - for this recipe. It's worth the money. The dressing can be made ahead. If by chance it lasts that long, it may be refrigerated for up to 2 weeks.*

1/2 cup blue cheese, crumbled
3 tablespoons buttermilk
3 tablespoons sour cream
2 tablespoons mayonnaise
2 teaspoons white wine vinegar
1/2 teaspoon Worcestershire sauce

1/4 teaspoon granulated sugar
1/8 teaspoon garlic powder
1/8 teaspoon bottled hot sauce
1/8 teaspoon kosher salt
1/8 teaspoon freshly ground black pepper

Mash blue cheese and buttermilk with a fork in a small, deep bowl until mixture resembles small curd cottage cheese. Add sour cream, mayonnaise, vinegar, Worcestershire sauce, sugar, garlic powder, hot sauce, salt, and pepper; stir well. Spoon into a glass jar, cover, and refrigerate.

# Dill Ranch Dressing

*Makes 2 cups*

*As the anointed dill queen at our house, this has my finest recommendation.*

1 cup mayonnaise
3/4 cup sour cream
1/4 cup buttermilk
1/4 cup onions, chopped
1 clove fresh garlic, minced

1 teaspoon cider vinegar
1/4 cup (packed) chopped parsley
2 tablespoons dried dill weed
3/4 teaspoon kosher salt
1/2 teaspoon freshly ground black pepper

Place all ingredients in the blender; pulse for a few seconds until smooth. Cover, and refrigerate several hours before serving.

# Easy French Dressing

*Makes 3 cups*

*Easy to make, tangy dressing with no preservatives as in the store-bought variety.*

1 cup canola oil
1/2 cup yellow onions, diced
1/2 cup ketchup
1/2 cup sugar
1/3 cup white wine vinegar

2 1/2 tablespoons lemon juice
1 teaspoon dry mustard
1 teaspoon sweet Hungarian paprika
1/2 teaspoon kosher salt
1/4 teaspoon freshly ground black pepper

Combine oil, onions, ketchup, sugar, vinegar, and lemon juice in a blender. Add mustard, paprika, salt, and pepper. Process until mixture is thick and smooth (about 2 minutes). Pour into glass container, cover, and refrigerate until needed.

# Fresh Herb Vinaigrette

*Makes 1 1/2 cups*

*Excellent with greens and and fresh produce.*

1/2 cup fresh basil leaves
2 tablespoons fresh parsley
2 tablespoons fresh marjoram
1 tablespoon fresh dill
2 cloves fresh garlic
2 teaspoons minced shallots
1/2 cup red wine vinegar
1/2 teaspoon kosher salt
1/8 teaspoon freshly ground black pepper
2/3 cup canola oil

Combine basil, parsley, marjoram, dill, garlic, shallots, vinegar, salt, and pepper in a blender or food processor; process until smooth. Gradually add oil; pulse a few seconds to blend well.


# Fresh Raspberry Vinaigrette

*Makes about 2/3 cup*

*An easy, great tasting dressing to be used on a variety of salads.*

1/3 cup canola oil
2 1/2 tablespoons raspberry vinegar
1/3 cup fresh or frozen raspberries
1 tablespoon shallots, chopped
1/2 teaspoon granulated sugar
1/2 teaspoon kosher salt

Place oil, vinegar, raspberries, shallots, sugar, and salt in a food processor or blender. Pulse for just a few seconds until all ingredients are well blended.

Pour dressing into a glass jar, cover tightly, and refrigerate at least 2 hours before using.

COOKING WITH CONFIDENCE

# Orange Dijon Dressing

*Makes 1 cup*

*Smooth orange flavor.*

1/4 cup frozen orange juice concentrate
1/4 cup white wine vinegar
1/4 cup shallots, chopped
2 tablespoons Dijon mustard
1/4 teaspoon kosher salt
18 teaspoon freshly ground black pepper
3/4 cup canola oil

Combine all except oil in blender; process until smooth. Gradually add oil to blend.

# Poppyseed Dressing

*Makes about 1 1/2 cups*

*Perfect on salad made with romaine lettuce, fresh strawberries, grilled chicken breast, chopped walnuts, and crumbled gorgonzola OR one made with greens, strawberries, toasted pecans, and crumbled bacon.*

3/4 cup granulated sugar
1/3 cup white wine vinegar
1/3 cup canola oil
1/3 cup chopped mild onion
1/2 teaspoon dry mustard
1 1/2 tablespoons poppy seeds

Combine sugar, vinegar, oil, onion, and mustard in a small bowl or food processor. Whisk vigorously or pulse briefly to mix well. Stir in poppy seeds. Cover tightly and refrigerate until needed.

# Raspberry Dressing

*Makes 2 cups*

*Wonderful on any salad with fruit in it.*

1 (10-ounce) frozen raspberries in syrup, thawed
2 tablespoons raspberry vinegar
1/4 cup canola oil
1/2 teaspoon prepared mustard
1/4 teaspoon kosher salt
3 tablespoons heavy cream

Place all ingredients in a blender. Pulse for a few seconds until smooth.

# Scoops of Confidence
## For Soups and Salads

Use an unbleached coffee filter inside a fine mesh strainer to **strain stocks** and **sauces**.

When your recipe calls for diced **tomatoes** and you have whole, canned tomatoes in your pantry, dip your kitchen shears right in the can and snip them to a desired size.

Three ways to keep **nuts** crunchy in your salad: (1) **toast** and stir in a skillet over medium heat until light brown and fragrant, or on a baking sheet at 350 degree oven for 10-15 minutes, (2) **glaze in** a skillet over medium low heat, stirring constantly, with 1 tablespoon of honey, until browned and completely coated; turn the nuts out on a glass plate or waxed paper to cool before using, and (3) **add** them to your salad just before serving.

Perfect **carrot matchsticks** for slaw? Cut flat "ribbons" with a wide peeler. Stack the ribbons, and cut into strips. Squaring off sides of any vegetable before slicing or dicing will result in uniform cuts.

When **choosing fruit**, remember the heavier fruit will be juicier. Before **extracting juice**, heat fruit for a few seconds in the microwave (don't cook it!) and roll it around a bit to activate its juice.

Peel tough skin from **broccoli stems**. Cut any "woody" parts away; slice on the diagonal and use in salads. Pretty, practical, crunchy.

If you use dried **rosemary**, grind it up first to release its natural oils and flavor.

To speed up the ripening of **avocados**, place in a perforated paper bag with an unpeeled apple. Close the bag and leave at room temperature for 2-3 days. To check for ripeness, insert a toothpick  If the pick goes in easily and comes out clean, it is ripe.

Wash **salad greens** and place them separately on a clean cotton dishtowel. Roll up the towel; place in it in a gallon ziptop bag and refrigerate. The dampness from the towel rehydrates the greens and keeps them crisp.

*Shrimp Pasta Salad*

PAGE 133

*Pumpkin and Lemon Tea Breads*

PAGES 55 – 56

*Focaccia Sandwiches*

PAGES 46 – 47

# Chicken Wild Rice Soup

PAGE 70

Butterscotch Pecan Cake

PAGE 160

*Buttermilk Doughnuts*

PAGE 45

*Walleye Cakes*

*Scallops Supreme*

PAGE 29

*Pizza from Scratch*

PAGES 119 – 120

*Greens with Fruit and Cheese*

PAGE 83

Lemon Cream Cheese Cake

PAGE 163

*Parmesan Chicken*

PAGE 139

Fresh Tomato Tart

PAGE 36

*Ginger Snaps from the Farm*
*Double Chocolate Cherry Cookies*
*Crispy Sugars*

PAGES 183, 184 AND 186

## Flourless Chocolate Cake

PAGE 162

# Corn and Black Bean Salsa

PAGE 22

*Origanum vulgare*
(Oregano)

# Pasta, Pizza, Rice

Bountiful Garden Pasta
Cajun Chicken Pasta
Spaetzle
Spaghetti Pie

Pizza from Scratch
Red Pizza Sauce
Pizza Toppings

Smorgasbord Rice
Rice Pilaf
Wild Rice Casserole

Scoops of Confidence

COOKING WITH CONFIDENCE

# Bountiful Garden Pasta

*6-8 servings*

*When tomatoes are in abundance...*

1 tablespoon olive oil
1 1/2 cups red onions, cut in strips
2 large cloves garlic, minced
1 pound spiced sausage, crumbled
1 pound penne pasta
1 cup dry white wine
2 large fresh tomatoes, cored and chopped
1 cup zucchini, cut in 1/4-inch slices
1/2 cup basil leaves, snipped in small pieces
Kosher salt
Freshly ground black pepper
Freshly grated Parmesan cheese

Cook pasta according to directions on the package.

Heat olive oil in large skillet over medium heat. Add onion; cook and stir 3 minutes. Stir in garlic and crumbled sausage; cook about 8 minutes or until sausage is no longer pink; drain. Add wine to skillet and cook to reduce volume by half. Stir in tomatoes; cook 5 minutes until the tomatoes soften and blend. Add zucchini slices; cook 1 additional minute.

Just before serving, stir in basil. Taste, and season with salt and pepper. (The amount will depend on the type of sausage used). Drain pasta; top with sauce, and serve. Garnish with Parmesan cheese.

# Cajun Chicken Pasta

*6-8 servings*

*Some like it hot...*

**1 pound linguine**

**3 boneless, skinless chicken breasts, cut into 1"cubes**

**5 tablespoons butter, divided**

**1/2 teaspoon Hungarian paprika, divided**

**1/2 teaspoon cayenne pepper, divided**

**2 large cloves garlic, minced**

**1/2 cup green onions, chopped**

**2 Roma tomatoes, seeded and chopped**

**1 cup celery, diced**

**1/2 red bell pepper, chopped**

**8 ounces mushrooms, chopped**

**1 1/2 cup heavy cream**

**1/2 cup dry sherry**

**1 tablespoon granular chicken bouillon**

**1/2 cup grated Asiago cheese**

**1/2 teaspoon bottled hot sauce**

*Garnish:*

**Red pepper flakes**

**Freshly grated Asiago cheese**

Cook pasta according to directions on the package.

Melt 3 tablespoons butter in large skillet over medium heat. Stir in 1/4 teaspoon paprika and 1/4 teaspoon cayenne pepper. Add chicken pieces; cook until browned and no longer pink in the center. Transfer chicken to a plate. Add remaining butter and garlic to the skillet. Stir in onion, and tomatoes; cook until tomatoes become tender and begin to blend. Add celery, red bell pepper and mushrooms; cook and stir for 3 minutes. Stir in cream, sherry, remaining paprika and cayenne pepper, chicken bouillon, cheese, and hot sauce; cook for about 2 additional minutes until well blended. Add reserved chicken; simmer for 2 minutes or until sauce is piping hot.

To serve, spoon sauce over cooked pasta. Garnish with red pepper flakes and Asiago cheese.

COOKING WITH CONFIDENCE

# Spaetzle

*Spaetzle are tiny noodles or dumplings. I learned how to make this dish from the cooks in Saarbrücken, Germany, and like to serve it with pork medallions and a flavorful sauce or gravy. It's really kind of messy but fun to make. After trying about 6 different devices to get the batter into the kettle, I found a specialty spaetzle maker or a flat, large-holed grater to work the best. Spaetzle can be made ahead, refrigerated, and finished at the last minute.*

**4 eggs, beaten**
**1/3 cup milk or water**
**2 tablespoons parsley, minced**
**1/2 teaspoon kosher salt**
**1/4 teaspoon nutmeg**
**2 cups all-purpose flour**
**2 quarts chicken broth or salted water**
**2 tablespoons clarified butter**

Whisk beaten eggs, milk, parsley, salt, and nutmeg together in a medium bowl. Add flour; whisk until batter adheres to the whisk. Let batter stand 15-20 minutes.

Bring chicken stock or water to a boil in a large, heavy saucepan. Coat all surfaces of the spaetzle maker or grater with non-stick vegetable spray. Push the batter through the spaetzle maker or grater into the boiling broth; simmer for 2 minutes. Using a slotted spoon, remove spaetzle from the broth and transfer to a colander. Rinse with cold water and drain well.

Transfer cold spaetzle to a towel-lined large baking pan or tray. Cover with another towel; refrigerate until needed. Note: Cleanup is so much easier if your bowl and utensils go straight to a cold water soak.

Just before serving, toss the spaetzle with clarified butter to coat well. Cook and stir in a large skillet over medium heat until spaetzle heats through and just begins to brown. Serve immediately.

# Spaghetti Pie

*Makes 6 servings*

*A yummy and different way to eat your spaghetti. Serve with a green salad and a great glass of wine.*

## Crust:
6 ounces spaghetti
1/2 cup grated Parmesan cheese
2 eggs, beaten
2 tablespoons butter

## Sauce and Topping:
3/4 pound ground beef
3/4 pound ground pork
1/2 cup chopped onion
1 (15-ounce) can diced tomatoes, undrained
1 (6-ounce) can tomato paste
1 teaspoon granulated sugar
1 1/2 teaspoons dried oregano
3/4 teaspoon garlic powder
1 3/4 cups ricotta cheese (or cottage cheese)
1 cup shredded mozzarella cheese
1 cup shredded provolone cheese

Preheat oven to 350 degrees. Butter a deep 10-inch pie plate; set aside.

Cook spaghetti as directed on the package; drain. Add Parmesan cheese, butter, and beaten eggs; mix well. Pat the spaghetti evenly around the sides and over the bottom of the prepared pie plate to form the crust.

Cook and stir the beef, pork, and onions in a skillet over medium heat until meat is no longer pink; drain off excess fat. Stir in tomatoes, tomato paste, sugar, oregano, and garlic powder; bring mixture to a simmer.

To complete pie assembly, spread ricotta evenly over the spaghetti crust. Spoon the beef mixture on top of the ricotta layer. Top with the two cheeses. Bake, uncovered, for 40 minutes. Allow the pie to rest for 10 minutes; cut in wedges and serve hot.

# Pizza from Scratch

*Caution: Once you know how to make pizza crust, you'll never be quite satisfied with take-out or delivery. Because rapid rise yeast is used instead of the regular variety, your water needs to be a little warmer. Test the temperature to make sure. I know these directions are lengthy, but read them all the way through before you begin. The rolling and shaping method is really fun, and your hands stay clean too.*

## Crust:
**1 2/3 cups all-purpose flour**
**1/3 cup semolina (pasta flour)**
**1 teaspoon rapid rise yeast**
**1 teaspoon granulated sugar**
**1/2 teaspoon kosher salt**
**3 tablespoons extra virgin olive oil, divided**
**1 cup hot water (120-125 degrees)**

**cornmeal for rolling**

Whisk flours, yeast, sugar, and salt together in a large bowl. Add 2 tablespoons olive oil, and water that has been heated and tested for temperature with an instant-read thermometer; stir briskly until dough comes away from the bowl and adheres to your spoon. Turn it out onto a lightly floured board; knead until smooth and elastic (about 5-7 minutes). Allow dough to rest for 10 minutes. Clean your dough bowl and rinse it in hot water; towel dry and coat the inside with remaining tablespoon of oil. Transfer dough to the bowl, turning several times to completely coat it with oil. Seal bowl with plastic wrap; cover with a heavy towel. Allow to rise and double in size.

Adjust oven rack to its lowest position. If you have a pizza stone (they're wonderful!), place it on the rack. Preheat oven to 500 degrees. I like to form the crusts and bake them on parchment paper. Just tear off a large piece and dust it with a little cornmeal. Form a portion of the dough into a round, flattened disk, place it on the parchment, and cover with a large piece of plastic wrap. Use a rolling pin to shape a circle, and your hands to push it into place. Remove the plastic wrap, and form a rim around the edge. Dress with toppings. If you have a pizza peel, use it to slide the pizza (parchment and all) onto the baking stone. Bake about 10 minutes until crust is deep brown; pull it on to a baking sheet to remove it from the oven.

Should you wish to bake any portion of the dough at a later time, seal it in a heavy duty zip-top bag. Refrigerate and use within 2 days.

# Red Pizza Sauce

*Makes about 3 cups*

*Quickly made from regular pantry ingredients. Start to finish, it's ready in less than 20 minutes.*

2 tablespoons butter
1 tablespoon canola oil
1 cup onions, finely diced
1/3 cup green pepper, finely diced
4 cloves fresh garlic, minced
1 (15-ounce) can diced tomatoes
1 (8-ounce) can tomato sauce

1 (6-ounce) can tomato paste
1 tablespoon dried oregano
1 teaspoon dried parsley flakes
1/2 teaspoon black pepper
1/4 teaspoon dried savory
1/4 teaspoon dried marjoram
1/4 teaspoon dried thyme

Heat butter and oil in a skillet. Add onions and green pepper; cook and stir for 3 minutes or until onions are translucent. Stir in garlic, tomatoes, tomato sauce, tomato paste, oregano, parsley, pepper, savory, marjoram, and thyme. Simmer 10 minutes, stirring occasionally.

Spoon onto prepared pizza crust; spread evenly, and add desired toppings.

# Pizza Toppings

*When it comes to pizza toppings, you are limited only by your imagination. Following are suggestions. The first three are the 6-inch pizzas featured in photographs.*

**Wagon Wheel Pizza**: base of Red Pizza Sauce, sliced kielbasa on the outside of pizza, rolled prosciutto form "spokes" to the center, crumbled bacon in the center; topped with shredded provolone and shredded basil.

**Barbequed Chicken Pizza**: base of barbeque sauce, diced barbequed chicken, rings of red onion; topped with smoked gouda and sliced mozzarella.

**Garden Pizza:** base of alfredo sauce, sliced fresh tomatoes, chopped sun dried tomatoes, sliced portobello mushrooms, and black olives; topped with crumbled goat cheese and fresh basil.

**Seafood Pizza**: prebake crust brushed with olive oil for 8 minutes; add shrimp, bay scallops, sun dried tomatoes, minced garlic, and shallots, top with fresh basil, Parmesan, and mozzarella; bake additional 5 minutes.

COOKING WITH CONFIDENCE

# Smorgasbord Rice

*A great smorgasbord (buffet) side dish. Another family favorite especially loved by my brother Kenny. The kids ask, "Is Mom making the rice?" whenever they're headed for home. Directions may seem lengthy; however, you'll make this confidently and quickly after the first time. It's also the only recipe I know of that stretches 1 cup of rice to feed 10 to 12 people.*

## Rice Pudding:
**1 cup regular rice, uncooked**
**6 cups water**
**4 cups milk**
**4 egg yolks**
**2 tablespoons cornstarch**
**1 cup granulated sugar**
**1 teaspoon pure almond extract**

## Meringue:
**4 egg whites**
**1/3 cup granulated sugar**
**1 teaspoon pure vanilla extract**

Preheat oven to 400 degrees.

For the pudding, combine uncooked rice and water in a large saucepan; bring to a boil. Cook for 10 minutes; drain water from the rice. Do not rinse. Transfer warm rice back to the saucepan. Add milk; heat to boiling once again. Cook, stirring often, for 5 minutes. Remove from heat.

Separate egg yolks from the whites, reserving the whites for meringue. In a small bowl, combine egg yolks and cornstarch. Gradually add about 1 cup of the hot rice and milk mixture to the cornstarch mixture and stir vigorously. Stir the warmed cornstarch mixture into the rice. Add sugar, salt, and almond extract; stir well. Return rice to the heat; cook and stir until slightly thickened. Transfer pudding to a 8 x 12-inch baking dish.

For the meringue, beat reserved egg whites until frothy. Add sugar and vanilla; continue beating until soft peaks form. Spread soft meringue evenly over pudding and tightly against the edges of the baking dish. Bake about 10 minutes or until meringue is light golden brown. Transfer to a wire rack and cool to room temperature, then refrigerate at least 3 hours. Cut in squares or scoop out for individual servings.

# Rice Pilaf

*Makes 6 servings*

*Here is an easy-to-prepare, tasty side dish that will soon become a family favorite.*

**6 tablespoons butter**
**2/3 cup onions, chopped**
**1/4 cup green pepper, finely chopped**
**1 cup (about 2 medium stalks) celery, finely chopped**
**1 cup uncooked rice**
**1/4 teaspoon dried thyme**
**1 (10 3/4-ounce) can low sodium chicken broth**
**1/2 teaspoon kosher salt**
**1/4 teaspoon freshly ground black pepper**

Preheat oven to 350 degrees.

Melt 3 tablespoons butter in a large skillet. Add onions, green pepper, and celery; cook and stir over medium heat until onions are translucent and fork-tender. Spoon cooked vegetables from the skillet and set aside. Heat remaining butter in the same skillet. Add rice; cook and stir over low heat until rice has lightly browned. Return vegetables to the skillet; add thyme, and remove from heat.

Add enough water to broth to equal 2 cups; bring to a boil, and stir into the rice and vegetable mixture. Add salt and pepper.

Spoon rice and vegetable mixture into a 1 1/2-quart casserole. Bake 30-40 minutes until rice is tender and liquid has been absorbed. Serve immediately.

COOKING with CONFIDENCE

# Wild Rice Casserole

*A tasty side for roasted chicken or turkey. Here in Minnesota, we lovingly call this "hotdish" - which is any combination of food that includes at least one can of soup. I say "casserole" only for you out-of-state folks. You will find it easily converts to a main dish (see directions at the end of this recipe).*

**1 cup wild rice, uncooked**
**2 (14-ounce) cans low sodium chicken broth**
**6 tablespoons butter, divided**
**3/4 cup slivered almonds**
**1 cup celery, diced**
**1 cup onions, diced**
**8 ounces fresh mushrooms, sliced**
**2 teaspoons lemon juice**
**1/2 teaspoon kosher salt**
**1/4 teaspoon freshly ground black pepper**
**1 large clove garlic, minced**
**1 (10-ounce) can cream of chicken soup**
**1/2 cup dry white wine**
**3/4 cup dried cranberries (or raisins)**

Rinse rice several times until rinse water is clear. Cook in 4 cups water for 15 minutes; drain. Return rice to the saucepan; add chicken broth; cook additional 15 minutes or until rice is somewhat tender and kernels have started to pop open. Do not drain.

Preheat oven to 350 degrees. Coat a 2 1/2-quart baking dish with non-stick vegetable spray; set aside.

Melt 2 tablespoons butter in a large skillet. Add almonds; cook and stir over medium heat about 1 minute until golden brown. Remove almonds from skillet and set aside. Add remaining butter, celery, and onions to the skillet; cook and stir over medium heat for 2 minutes. Add mushrooms, lemon juice, salt, pepper, and garlic; cook additional 2 minutes. Stir in soup, wine, and cranberries. Transfer to prepared baking dish. Stir in cooked rice. Bake (uncovered) for 50 minutes; turn oven off, and let casserole rest for 20 minutes. Serve warm.

\* Note: This dish can be prepared ahead of time. Re-heat (covered) in a 325 degree oven for 30 minutes.

**Chicken Wild Rice Casserole**: Make Wild Rice Casserole as directed. Add 1 1/2 cups cubed, cooked chicken, and 1/2 cup milk. Using a 3-quart baking dish, bake 50 minutes in a 350 degree oven.

# Scoops of Confidence

## For Pasta, Pizza, Rice

**Pasta tips and techniques:**

Pasta can serve as a versatile lifeline at lunch or dinnertime. It is perhaps the most forgiving of all the staples you have on hand. Keep several varieties in your pantry. **Cooking water** should be salted and at a rolling boil before pasta is added. Add pasta; stir occasionally. To keep from overcooking, check the pasta a minute or two before it is scheduled to be done. Drain, but don't rinse; no oil is needed. If you are having problems with pasta sticking together or getting mushy, more than likely you have not started with enough water or have cooked it too long. Watch the directions on the package. Each brand has its own varieties, sizes, and shapes; cooking times will vary.

**Tips for pasta sauce:**

Thin out a sauce that's a little too thick with some of your pasta cooking water. Reheat sauced pasta for just a minute or so just before bringing to the table so the dish is piping hot.

**Pasta Name/Shapes**

**Cavatappi** /corkscrew      **Orecchette**/thumbprints
**Fusilli**/little springs      **Penne**/straight tubes, cut diagonally
**Farfalle**/bow ties      **Radiatore**/radiators
**Gemelli**/twists      **Rotelle**/wheels
**Mostaccioli**/little moustaches      **Ziti**/long thin tubes

**Rice:**

Match the **variety of rice** to the dish you are preparing: **short-grain** cooks up soft and sticky, and is best for sushi, rice puddings, and stir-fries. **Long-grain** cooks up fluffy, and is best for rice pilaf and salads. Properties of the starches in each variety make the difference.

Tips for **Cooking Wild Rice**: Wash, wash, wash it many times until your water runs clean and clear. Cook it for 15 minutes, drain, and start over with clean water. Proceed to cook it for an additional 30-35 minutes or until kernels have started to pop open. It is not meant to be served while still in the black, closed kernel stage.

*Pomoxis nigromaculatus*

(Black Crappie)

# Fish and Seafood

Apple Baked Tilapia
Italian Walleye
Walleye Cakes
Mustard Sauced Salmon

Seafood Extraordinaire
Shrimp Pasta Salad
Shrimp that Sizzles

Scoops of Confidence

# Apple Baked Tilapia

*4 servings*

Farm raised tilapia is gaining in popularity because of its mild, sweet taste. I like to serve this with a side of rice or pasta. Make the sauce and cook the rice or pasta while the fish is baking, and you're ready to serve this in 20 minutes.

4 tilapia fillets (or substitute mild white fish such as grouper, cod, or flounder)
1/4 teaspoon kosher salt
1/8 teaspoon freshly ground black pepper
5 tablespoons butter, divided
1/3 cup dry white wine
3/4 cup onions, thinly sliced
2 1/2 cups fresh apples, cored and sliced
1/2 cup Calvados apple brandy (or apple cider)
1 cup heavy cream
1/2 teaspoon dried basil
1/2 teaspoon kosher salt
1/4 teaspoon freshly ground black pepper
1 1/2 cups rice (or pasta), cooked according to directions on the package

Preheat oven to 400 degrees. Sprinkle salt and pepper over fish fillets; arrange in a 2 quart shallow baking dish.

Melt 2 tablespoons butter in a small saucepan; add wine and boil for 1 minute. Pour butter sauce over fish. Bake 15 minutes or until fish is opaque.

While fish is baking, cook rice or pasta according to package directions. For the sauce, heat 3 tablespoons of butter in a skillet. Add onions; cook and stir over medium heat for 3 minutes. Add sliced apples and apple brandy; cook 3 minutes on low heat, stirring occasionally. Stir in cream, basil, salt, and pepper.

To serve, spoon rice or pasta onto individual plates. Place fish fillet along side, and top with sauce.

# *Italian Baked Walleye*

*4-6 servings*

*I have a reputation at our house for catching the "bakers" - fish that are large and thick - and this is one of my favorite ways to present them. Here is a dish that looks like you spent hours instead of just minutes to prepare.*

**3 or 4 large walleye fillets (or other firm whitefish) to fit baking dish**
**5 or 6 fresh tomatoes**
**2 cups seasoned Italian breadcrumbs**
**Kosher salt to taste**
**Freshly ground black pepper to taste**
**3/4 cup dry white wine**
**6 tablespoons butter**
**2 teaspoons fresh lemon juice**
**2 cups freshly grated Parmesan cheese**
**Sweet Hungarian paprika for sprinkling on top**
**1 lemon - to be squeezed on the top**

Preheat oven to 500 degrees. Yes, this is the right temperature.

Butter a 13 x 9 x 2-inch glass baking dish. Slice tomatoes very thinly; cover entire bottom of the dish with the slices. Sprinkle breadcrumbs evenly over the sliced tomatoes. Place the fish fillets in a single layer to completely cover the breadcrumbs; sprinkle with salt and pepper.

In a small saucepan, combine wine, butter, and lemon juice. Bring to a boil; cook for 3 minutes. Stir well; pour hot mixture over the fish. Distribute Parmesan cheese evenly, covering the fish. Sprinkle with paprika, and squeeze lemon juice over the top. Bake 10-20 minutes, or until fish is opaque.

COOKING WITH CONFIDENCE

# Walleye Cakes

*My "Northwoods" creation, perhaps destined to become one of your family favorites.*

**1 pound uncooked walleye (bones removed) or other firm, white fish**
      **to equal about 3 cups, packed**
**1/4 cup onions, minced**
**1 1/2 tablespoons Old Bay seasoning**
**1 tablespoon fresh parsley, minced**
**1 tablespoon fresh thyme, minced**
**1/2 teaspoon dill weed**
**1/4 teaspoon coarsely ground black pepper**
**1 large clove garlic, minced**
**1 cup fresh bread crumbs\*, soaked in milk and squeezed dry**
**1 egg, beaten**
**1/3 cup cold milk, mixed with 2 tablespoons cornstarch**

## Crust:
**2/3 cup blanched almonds, ground**
**2/3 cup fresh bread crumbs**

**4 tablespoons clarified butter\*\* for frying**

Using a food processor with a metal blade, coarsely chop the uncooked fish. Toss fish, onion, Old Bay, parsley, thyme, dill, pepper, and garlic together in a large bowl until well mixed. Add bread crumbs, egg, and cornstarch mixture; stir lightly to combine. Form the patties by lightly packing a 1/4 cup dry measuring cup for the large, or a 1 1/2-inch scoop for the appetizer-size. Flatten each patty slightly to make about a 3 1/2-inch round for the large serving size, or a 2-inch round for the small.

For the crust, mix ground almonds and bread crumbs; completely coat all surfaces of the patties. Heat clarified butter\*\* in a large, heavy skillet. Cook patties at medium high heat (about 3 minutes on each side) until nicely browned. Note: Patties can be formed ahead of time and finished just before serving, OR browned and baked for 8-10 minutes in a 350 degree oven. Serve hot with your choice of dipping sauces.

\*        For bread crumbs, remove the crusts from a few slices of firm, white bread. Tear slices into large pieces; pulse a few seconds in a food processor or blender to a fine crumb consistency.

\*\*      For clarified butter, melt 6 tablespoons butter over medium heat in a small saucepan. Skim accumulated foam from the top. Pour off the clear (clarified) butter; discard white milk solids left behind. Because of its high smoking point, using clarified butter results in a golden brown crust.

# Mustard Sauced Salmon

*4 servings*

*Although some marinating time is required, actual cooking time from start to finish is under 20 minutes, resulting in a dish that presents beautifully and tastes fabulous.*

**4 salmon steaks**

*Marinade:*
**1 cup dry white wine**
**1 cup milk**

*Mustard Sauce:*
**1 1/3 cups sour cream**
**2/3 cup green onions, finely sliced**
**1 3/4 tablespoons Dijon mustard**
**1 1/2 tablespoons fresh parsley, minced**
**3/4 teaspoon dried thyme**
**3/4 teaspoon dried marjoram**
**1/2 teaspoon dried dill weed**
**1/4 teaspoon kosher salt**
**1/4 teaspoon freshly ground black pepper**

**Additional salt and black pepper for broiling**

Remove skin from salmon steaks. For the marinade, combine wine and milk in a shallow glass container. Add salmon; marinate for 30 minutes, turning occasionally.

For the mustard sauce, combine sour cream, onions, mustard, parsley, thyme, marjoram, dill, salt, and pepper in a small bowl. Stir well; set aside to allow flavors to blend.

Preheat broiler. Line a baking sheet with foil; coat lightly with non-stick vegetable spray. Drain the steaks and pat dry with a paper towel; place on prepared pan. Sprinkle both sides of the steaks lightly with salt and pepper. Broil 6 inches below the heat for 7 minutes. Remove from broiler, turn the steaks, and spread the reserved mustard sauce evenly on each of the top sides. Return to broil an additional 4-5 minutes or until salmon is firm and opaque. Depending on the thickness of the steaks, broiling time may vary. Just take care not to overcook. Serve immediately.

# Seafood Extraordinaire

*Perhaps the most popular of the kitchen creations at our house, this is the one we all call special.*

**2 tablespoons clarified butter**
**1 tablespoon canola oil**
**2/3 cup onions, finely diced**
**1 cup celery, finely diced**
**1 pound mushrooms, sliced**
**1/4 teaspoon freshly ground black pepper**
**1 pound medium shrimp, cooked with 1/2 teaspoon Old Bay seasoning**
**Season shrimp with 1/2 teaspoon Old Bay and 1 teaspoon fresh lemon juice**
**1 pound bay scallops, dusted with all-purpose flour, salt, and pepper**
**1 pound cooked crabmeat**
**2 cups half and half**
**1 1/2 tablespoons granulated chicken bouillon**
**1/2 teaspoon each: dried basil, dried dill weed, and Old Bay seasoning**
**2/3 cup freshly grated Parmesan cheese and 1/4 cup grated Romano cheese**
**1 cup dry white wine**
**Fresh Parmesan cheese and parsley for garnish**
**1 pound fettuccine**

Heat butter and oil in a large skillet. Add onions and celery; cook and stir over medium heat for 3 minutes until translucent. Add mushrooms and pepper; cook and stir additional 2 minutes.

Bring water to a rolling boil in a large pot. Add shrimp and Old Bay to the water. Cook until water returns to a boil; drain, and immediately rinse with cold water. Toss shrimp with Old Bay and fresh lemon juice.

Add scallops to the skillet; cook for 2 minutes until they start turning opaque. Immediately add cooked shrimp and crabmeat to the skillet. Stir in cream, bouillon, basil, dill, Old Bay, and both cheeses. Add wine; simmer on low heat for 3 minutes.

Cook fettuccine according to directions on the package; drain. Serve with seafood sauce, and garnish with Parmesan cheese and parsley.

# Shrimp that Sizzles

*The main feature for a perfect summer evening on the deck.*

**2 pounds large shrimp, fresh or frozen**

**<u>Marinade:</u>**
**1/4 cup brown sugar**
**1/4 cup lemon juice**
**1/4 cup vegetable oil**
**1/4 cup chile sauce**
**1 (8-ounce) can tomato sauce**
**2 tablespoons Worcestershire sauce**
**1 cup onion, finely chopped**
**3 cloves garlic, minced**
**1/4 cup dry white wine**
**1/2 teaspoon thyme**
**1/2 teaspoon parsley**
**1/2 teaspoon grated lemon peel**
**1/4 teaspoon celery seed**

For marinade, combine brown sugar, lemon juice, oil, chile sauce, tomato sauce, Worcestershire sauce, onion, and garlic in a saucepan over medium heat; bring to a boil. Reduce heat; stir occasionally, and simmer for 20 minutes. Stir in wine, thyme, parsley, lemon peel, and celery seed; simmer additional 10 minutes. Set aside to cool.

If shrimp are fresh: peel, devein, and rinse in cold water. If frozen: thaw in cold water, peel, devein, and refresh in lightly salted water for about 15 minutes; rinse with cold water. Butterfly the shrimp by cutting along the outside curve (but not all the way through), allowing the shrimp to open up and lay flat.

Spoon the cooled marinade into a heavy duty zip top plastic bag. Add shrimp; remove as much air as possible from the bag so shrimp is completely immersed in marinade. Close bag tightly; refrigerate for 1 hour.

Remove shrimp from marinade. Broil or grill about 4 inches away from direct heat until firm and pink, turning and basting shrimp with marinade at least once during the cooking process. Serve hot or cold.

# Shrimp Pasta Salad

*Fresh from the sea taste, pretty as a picture.*

**1 (8-ounce) package gemelli pasta**
**1 pound medium-sized shrimp, cooked**
**1/2 teaspoon Old Bay seasoning**
**1 teaspoon fresh lemon juice**
**1 cup celery, finely diced**
**1/4 cup red onion, finely diced**
**2 Roma tomatoes, seeded and finely diced**

*Dressing:*
**1/2 cup mayonnaise**
**1/3 cup plain yogurt**
**3 tablespoons fresh lemon juice**
**2 tablespoons heavy cream**
**2 tablespoons white wine vinegar**
**1 tablespoon Dijon mustard**
**1/2 teaspoon Old Bay seasoning**
**1 teaspoon dried dill weed**
**3/4 teaspoon kosher salt**
**1/2 teaspoon freshly ground black pepper**
**Fresh parsley for garnish**

Cook pasta according to directions on the package; drain, and cool. Rinse and drain cooked shrimp; transfer to a medium bowl. Toss shrimp with Old Bay and lemon juice; set a few shrimp aside for garnish.

In a large bowl, combine the cooked pasta with celery, onion, and tomatoes. For the dressing, whisk the mayonnaise, yogurt, lemon juice, cream, vinegar, mustard, Old Bay, dill, salt, and pepper together in a small bowl until smooth. Stir the dressing into the pasta mixture; add seasoned shrimp and mix well. Garnish with parsley and reserved shrimp.

# Scoops of Confidence

## For Fish and Seafood

There is a perfect wine for every food and sauce. Since it is used so often in fish and seafood dishes, here are my thoughts on the subject: **Wine chosen for cooking** should be one you would otherwise drink and enjoy, as cooking concentrates the wine's flavor. One labeled "cooking wine" will not assure optimum results for your kitchen masterpieces. Take a whiff; you would not drink that stuff. Instead, read the helpful information on a real wine bottle label and/or ask your wine merchant for assistance.

### Shrimp Tips:

When purchasing, choose firm, sweet-smelling shrimp. If they smell like iodine, leave them at the market.

To stop the cooking process, drain the shrimp and immediately plunge them into ice water.

Do not overcook - the taste will disappear, and the shrimp will be tough and rubbery.

### Fish Tips:

When purchasing or processing fish, make sure it has no distinct smell. If it smells fishy, it will taste fishy.

Maximum time for **marinating fish**? About 30 minutes. Much longer, and flavor of the fish is compromised.

Remove fish from the heat before it is totally done. It will continue to cook a bit from its own heat. As a general rule, **cook 4-5 minutes per ½-inch thickness**. When it's done, fish juices should be milky white in color, and flesh should be opaque.

Make your own **Savory Butter** for fish:
Whip 1/2 pound of soft butter. Add 2 1/2 tablespoons minced sun-dried tomatoes, 1 teaspoon minced shallots, 3/4 teaspoon fresh lemon juice, 1/2 teaspoon dried thyme, and 1/4 teaspoon minced fresh thyme. Stir well; drizzle over broiled fish fillets. Any unused butter should be refrigerated in an airtight container.

*Gallus Gallus*

*(Feather of an English Buff Orpington Chicken)*

# Poultry, Meat, Game

Chicken Marsala
Orange Chicken and Rice
Parmesan Chicken
Pulled Barbequed Beef
Steak Stroganoff
Swedish Meatballs

Barbequed Ribs
Pork Roast with Mustard Sauce
Rosemary Pork Medallions

Gourmet Goose
Pheasant Supreme

On Making Gravy

Scoops of Confidence

# Chicken Marsala

*Often enjoyed in a restaurant setting, Chicken Marsala is easy to duplicate in your own kitchen.*

**4 skinless, boneless chicken breasts**
**1 teaspoon kosher salt**
**1/4 teaspoon freshly ground black pepper**
**1/2 cup all-purpose flour**
**2 tablespoons canola oil**
**3 tablespoons clarified butter**

*Sauce:*
**3/4 cup thinly sliced onions**
**8 ounces fresh mushrooms, quartered**
**2 cloves garlic, thinly sliced**
**1 1/2 cups Marsala wine, divided**
**1 cup low sodium chicken broth**
**1 1/2 tablespoons fresh lemon juice**
**1 1/2 teaspoons cornstarch**
**1/4 cup heavy cream**

*Garnish:*
**2 tablespoons fresh parsley, minced**

Preheat oven to 350 degrees. Coat a 1 1/2-quart baking dish with non-stick vegetable spray; set aside.

Cut the chicken breasts in half horizontally; flatten between 2 sheets of plastic to an even thickness. Mix salt and pepper in a small dish; sprinkle lightly over all surfaces of the chicken pieces. Dredge seasoned chicken in flour to coat evenly. Heat oil and butter in skillet until very hot. Add chicken pieces; brown on both sides, and transfer to the prepared baking dish.

For sauce, add onions to the skillet; cook and stir over medium heat for 2 minutes. Add mushrooms and garlic; cook and stir about 5 minutes or until liquid from mushrooms has evaporated. Stir in 1 cup of the wine and chicken broth. Simmer 3-4 minutes until sauce has reduced in volume. Mix lemon juice, remaining wine and cornstarch. Whisk into the sauce to thicken. Simmer 3 minutes. Add cream; stir well. Pour sauce over chicken.

Bake 35 minutes. Serve over spaetzle, buttered noodles, or mashed potatoes. Garnish with minced parsley.

# Orange Chicken and Rice

*6 servings*

*Wonderful served with warm biscuits and a green salad.*

**6 boneless, skinless chicken breasts**
**4 tablespoons butter**
**2 tablespoons all-purpose flour**
**1/4 teaspoon kosher salt**
**1/8 teaspoon cinnamon**
**1/8 teaspoon cloves**
**1 1/2 cups orange juice**
**1/4 teaspoon bottled hot sauce**
**3/4 cup slivered almonds**
**1/2 cup golden raisins**
**1 large (15-ounce) can mandarin orange segments, drained**

*Rice:*
**2 cups long-grained rice, cooked**
**4 tablespoons frozen orange juice concentrate, thawed**

Preheat oven to 350 degrees. Coat a 2 1/2 quart casserole with non-stick vegetable spray; set aside.

For the chicken, melt butter in a large skillet over medium high heat. Add chicken breasts; brown on both sides. Transfer chicken to prepared casserole. Add flour, salt, cinnamon, and cloves to butter remaining in skillet; stir to a smooth consistency. Whisk in orange juice and hot sauce; cook and whisk until mixture thickens and comes to a boil. Add almonds and raisins; spoon over chicken in the casserole. Cover, and bake for 35 minutes. Remove from oven; stir in orange segments. Return to the oven for 5 minutes.

For the rice, cook according to package directions. Remove from heat; stir in orange juice concentrate.

To serve, place a portion of the rice on each plate. Place a chicken breast on top of the rice, and spoon orange sauce over all.

# Parmesan Chicken

*Such an easy dish to prepare, and so delicious to serve.*

**6 boneless, skinless chicken breasts**
**1 cup fresh bread crumbs***
**1 cup grated Parmesan cheese**
**1/4 cup finely chopped fresh parsley (or 1 tablespoon dried)**
**1/4 teaspoon garlic powder**
**3/4 teaspoon kosher salt**
**1/2 teaspoon black pepper**
**4 tablespoons butter, melted**
**1/2 teaspoon paprika**

Preheat oven to 350 degrees. Line a jelly roll pan or large baking sheet with foil; coat lightly with vegetable oil spray and set aside.

Combine bread crumbs, Parmesan cheese, parsley, garlic powder, salt, and pepper in a large bowl; mix well, and set aside. Rinse chicken breasts in cold water and pat dry with a paper towel. Dip chicken in melted butter, taking care to cover thoroughly. Dredge butter-covered chicken in the crumb mixture to coat well. Let prepared chicken rest for 15 minutes, allowing breading to partially dry.

Place chicken pieces 2-3 inches apart on prepared pan. Bake for 50 minutes or until chicken is tender. You won't want to turn the breasts while baking --- they will be crispy and golden brown when done. Sprinkle with paprika; serve with roasted vegetables.

\*      To prepare fresh bread crumbs, cut the crusts off firm, white bread. Pulse in food processor until consistency of crumbs.

# Pulled Barbequed Beef

*Approximately 10 servings*

*This is the beef that accompanies my hunters to "deer camp" each Fall. Although I have used this basic recipe for a number of years, I have also been known to add barbeque sauce, a little mustard, more bourbon, more anything it tasted like it needed at the time. Follow the recipe; then just taste, and experiment a little. Note the marinating and slow roasting times to plan accordingly.*

**1 (about 5-pound) beef roast**

*Marinade:*
**1/3 cup good quality bourbon whiskey**
**1 tablespoon molasses**
**1/4 cup low sodium soy sauce**
**1 1/2 teaspoons kosher salt**
**1 teaspoon peppercorns**
**4 cloves fresh garlic**
**1 1/2 cups onions, chopped**
**2 large stalks celery, chopped**

Cut beef roast into several pieces; place in a gallon-size, heavy duty zip-top bag; set aside. For marinade, place whiskey, molasses, soy sauce, salt, peppercorns, garlic, chopped onions, and chopped celery in a blender; pulse a few times until mixture is no longer chunky. Pour marinade over the beef, remove as much air from the bag as possible, seal, and refrigerate for at least 12 hours.

Preheat oven to 200 degrees. Remove beef from the bag and place it on a large sheet of heavy duty foil. Fold up all sides of the foil. Pour marinade over the top of the beef and fold the foil over all, sealing tightly. Place the sealed "package" in an open baking pan. Bake 10-12 hours, or until beef seemingly falls apart.

Transfer cooked beef to another shallow pan. With a fork in each hand, pull the beef apart in shreds. Add all juices to the shredded beef. It will look like there's too much juice; however, the meat will reabsorb most of it. Serve hot on hearty buns with Creamy Horseradish Sauce.

**Creamy Horseradish Sauce**: Combine 1 1/4 cups mayonnaise, 1/4 cup sour cream, 1/4 cup prepared horseradish, 1 1/2 teaspoons fresh lemon juice, and 1/4 teaspoon bottled hot sauce. Stir well; cover, and chill.

COOKING WITH CONFIDENCE

# Steak Stroganoff

*4 servings*

*A hearty treat on a chilly evening at the lake.*

1 1/2 pounds sirloin or chuck steak, cut into 3/4-inch cubes
1 cup all-purpose flour
1 1/2 teaspoons kosher salt
1/2 teaspoon freshly ground black pepper
1 tablespoon canola oil
1 tablespoon butter
3/4 cup minced onions
1/2 pound fresh mushrooms, quartered
1 large clove garlic, minced
1 (14-ounce) can low sodium beef broth
2 teaspoons granular beef bouillon
1 1/2 tablespoons tomato paste
1 tablespoon Worcestershire sauce
1/2 teaspoon bottled hot sauce
1/2 teaspoon kosher salt

Combine flour, salt, and pepper in a small bowl. Add beef cubes; coat well. Heat oil and butter in a Dutch oven or large skillet. Add beef; cook and stir until brown. Add onions, mushrooms, garlic, beef broth, bouillon, tomato paste, Worcestershire, hot sauce, and salt. Simmer over very low heat for 45 minutes, stirring occasionally.

Serve over spaetzle or hot buttered noodles.

# Swedish Meatballs

*6 servings*

*Folks of Swedish ancestry are quite well represented in the Midwest. Because they are known to eat what so many of us call "white food", I thought it appropriate to give credit to their meatballs and (almost white) gravy. Just a little different seasoning makes these a special treat.*

## Meatballs:
1 1/2 pounds lean ground beef
1 1/2 pounds ground pork
4 tablespoons butter
1 1/2 cups minced onions
2 eggs
1 cup milk
1 tablespoon granulated sugar
2 1/2 teaspoons kosher salt
1 teaspoon allspice
1 teaspoon nutmeg
1 cup fresh breadcrumbs

## White Gravy:
Fat drippings from the skillet
2 tablespoons butter
6 tablespoons all-purpose flour
1 teaspoon granulated sugar
1/8 teaspoon white pepper
2 cups water
1 1/2 cups half and half
1 teaspoon dried parsley

Preheat oven to 350 degrees.

For the meatballs, heat butter in skillet. Add onions; cook and stir until tender; transfer onions to a large bowl. Combine onions with beef, pork, eggs, milk, sugar, salt, allspice, and nutmeg. Mix all ingredients well. Add breadcrumbs; mix gently. Form into meatballs and place in a baking pan. Bake 30 minutes.

For the gravy, add butter to the skillet. Add flour, sugar, and pepper; cook and stir 3 minutes. Gradually whisk in water and cream until thick and smooth. Add meatballs to the gravy; simmer 10 minutes to blend flavors. Serve with mashed potatoes.

COOKING WITH CONFIDENCE

# Barbequed Ribs

*The list of components for ribs is long. But a visit to your pantry should make quick work of assembling a few bottles and cans. Then just go for it. Begin preparing the ribs the day before serving.*

## Spice Rub and Ribs:
1/4 cup brown sugar
1 tablespoon kosher salt
1 1/2 teaspoons chili powder
1 1/2 teaspoons Hungarian paprika
1 1/2 teaspoons freshly ground pepper
1/2 teaspoon garlic powder
1/2 teaspoon freshly grated lemon rind
1/4 teaspoon ground cinnamon
8 pounds baby back pork ribs (about 4 whole racks)

## Barbeque Sauce:
| | |
|---|---|
| 2 1/2 tablespoons butter | 2 tablespoons Worcestershire sauce |
| 1 cup chopped onions | 2 tablespoons low sodium soy sauce |
| 3 cloves chopped fresh garlic | 2 tablespoons pure maple syrup |
| 1 cup water | 1 1/2 teaspoons liquid smoke |
| 1 3/4 cup ketchup | 3/4 teaspoon dry mustard |
| 3/4 cup bottled chili sauce | 3/4 teaspoon Hungarian paprika |
| 3 tablespoons lemon juice | 1/4 teaspoon kosher salt |
| 2 tablespoons brown sugar | 1/8 teaspoon freshly ground black pepper |
| | 1/8 teaspoon thyme |

For the sauce, melt butter in a Dutch oven or heavy skillet; add onions. Cook and stir for 3 minutes; remove from heat. Stir in all remaining ingredients; return pan to the heat. Bring to almost boiling; reduce heat and simmer for 10 minutes, stirring occasionally.

Place spice rub ingredients in a medium sized bowl or food processor; mix well.

(1) Trim the racks of ribs by trimming off excess fat that would start a fire when the ribs are on the grill. (2) Turn the rack of ribs over so you can see the bone side; pull off the tough membrane that covers the area. Why? Leaving it intact means your seasonings cannot penetrate the meat as well. It also makes the ribs chewy and difficult to eat. Just make a slit in the membrane close to the rib tip. With a paper towel in your hand (for grip), grasp one end of the membrane and pull it toward you. (3) Trim the skirt (the meat flap that extends beyond the bones). This can be grilled, but it's easier to handle it on its own. (4) Spread the ribs on both sides with spices and rub the surface (disposable gloves work great for this). (5) Stack up the ribs in a pan, cover, and refrigerate until tomorrow.

Long slow grilling is the answer to perfect ribs. Maintaining a temperature of 230 to 250 degrees for about 5 hours is ideal. Whether or not to coat the meat with sauce during the grilling process is a personal decision. I think it's easier to cook the ribs first, adding the sauce the last 30 minutes of grilling to caramelize.

# Pork Roast with Mustard Sauce

*6-8 servings*

*If you are looking for something special for a dinner party, this is it.*

**4 pounds center-cut, boneless pork loins, trimmed**

*Marinade:*
**1/2 cup low-sodium soy sauce**
**1/2 cup good quality bourbon whiskey**
**1/4 cup brown sugar**

*Mustard Sauce:*
**1/3 cup sour cream**
**1/3 cup mayonnaise**
**1 tablespoon dry mustard**
**1 tablespoon finely chopped shallots**
**1 1/2 teaspoons white wine vinegar**
**1/4 teaspoon kosher salt**
**1/8 teaspoon freshly ground pepper**

For marinade, combine soy sauce, bourbon and brown sugar; mix well to dissolve sugar. Trim pork roasts of all silverskin by gently cutting beneath the surface; pull skin away as you cut. Place trimmed roasts in a large, heavy-duty plastic zip top bag; pour marinade into the bag. Remove as much air from the bag as possible so you can see the meat is completely submerged in the marinade. Refrigerate 2-4 hours.

For Mustard Sauce, combine all ingredients; mix well.  Cover and refrigerate for several hours to allow flavors to blend.

Preheat oven to 300 degrees. Bring meat back to room temperature; place on rack in shallow pan.  Roast, basting frequently with marinade for two hours, or until meat thermometer inserted in thickest portion registers 155 degrees. Cover roast lightly with foil and allow to rest 15 minutes before slicing.  Serve with Mustard Sauce.

# Rosemary Pork Medallions

*4 servings*

*A flavorful main dish --- simple enough for everyday, special enough for guests.*

**1 pound boneless pork loin**
**Kosher salt and freshly ground pepper**
**3 tablespoons butter, divided**
**2 teaspoons canola oil**
**3/4 cup sun-dried tomatoes (not packed in oil)**
**1/4 cup onions, diced**
**4 large cloves fresh garlic, minced**
**1 cup nonfat chicken broth**
**1/3 cup dry white wine**
**1 1/2 tablespoons fresh rosemary, minced**

Place dried tomatoes in a small bowl; cover with boiling water. They will be soft enough to use in about 20 minutes.

Trim pork loin of all fat; slice into medallions about 1 inch thick. Place each piece between 2 pieces of plastic wrap or waxed paper and flatten to a uniform thickness of about 1/2 inch. Season both sides lightly with salt and pepper. Heat 1 tablespoon of the butter and oil in a heavy skillet; add pork slices. Cook about 2 minutes on each side. Transfer to a warm plate; cover with foil to keep hot.

Remove softened tomatoes from water. Place in food processor with about 1/2 cup of the broth; pulse until a thick, tomato paste-like mixture forms. Set aside.

Reheat skillet. Add onions, cooking and stirring over medium heat for about 2 minutes. Add garlic, tomato mixture, remaining broth, wine, and rosemary; simmer additional 3 minutes. Stir in remaining 2 tablespoons of butter.

To serve, place warm pork slice on plate. Top with a spoonful of rosemary sauce.

# Gourmet Goose

*4 servings*

*Hunters will delight in reaping the rewards of their bounty. This is an exceptional dish.*

**2 pounds wild goose breast fillets, sliced 1/2" thick**
**3 tablespoons butter**
**3 large carrots, peeled and sliced thin**
**2 cloves garlic, chopped**
**2/3 cup chopped onions**
**2 cups sliced fresh mushrooms**
**2 cups broccoli florets (about 1 medium bunch)**
**1 (6 ounce) can cream of mushroom soup**
**1/2 cup heavy cream**
**1 tablespoon granulated chicken bouillon**
**1/2 cup dry white wine**
**1/2 teaspoon kosher salt**
**1/4 teaspoon freshly ground black pepper**

Preheat oven to 350 degrees. Melt butter in large skillet; add goose fillets and brown on high heat. Transfer fillets to a heat-proof casserole. Add carrots to the skillet; stir fry until crisp-tender. Add garlic, onions and mushrooms; cook and stir over medium heat for additional 2 minutes. Add broccoli to the mixture; season with salt and pepper. Transfer vegetables to the casserole to surround the goose fillets. Stir soup, cream, wine and bouillon together in a bowl. Season with additional salt and pepper if desired. Pour mixture over the goose fillets and vegetables. Bake, uncovered, for 30 minutes.

# Pheasant Supreme

*8-10 servings*

*This was a favorite of ours at home on the farm, and great served with mashed potatoes.*

**3 pheasants, skinned, cleaned, and quartered**
**2 cups all-purpose flour**
**1/2 teaspoon kosher salt**
**1/4 teaspoon freshly ground pepper**
**1/8 teaspoon oregano**
**1/8 teaspoon thyme**
**1/8 teaspoon savory**
**1/8 teaspoon sage**
**2 tablespoons shortening**
**2 tablespoons butter**
**1 cup dry white wine**
**1 1/2 cups heavy cream**

Preheat oven to 350 degrees. Mix flour, salt, pepper, oregano, thyme, savory, and sage in a large, heavy-duty zip top bag. Add pheasant pieces, one at a time, and shake until well coated. Melt shortening and butter in heavy skillet. Brown pheasant pieces on all sides. Place browned pieces in a large baking pan; add white wine and cover tightly with aluminum foil. Bake 1 1/2 hours or until pheasant is fork-tender. Check periodically; add a little water to the pan if it appears to be too dry. Add cream; cover, and bake additional 30 minutes.

The cream, wine, and any juices from the pheasant stir together to make a great tasting gravy.

COOKING WITH CONFIDENCE

# ... On Making Gravy

One of the questions often asked is "How do I make good tasting, **lump-free gravy**?" Here are my thoughts on the subject:

Once your meat has finished cooking, whatever is left in the pan when the meat is removed can be used for the basic flavor. Scrape these bits and pieces (pan drippings) from the bottom of the pan, add broth or water (and some wine if desired), and taste. Add seasonings if needed. Taste again, because the flavor of your finished gravy totally depends on how good the broth tastes.

The biggest challenge for most people comes next: How do I **thicken** the broth to make gravy?

Use the formula:         2 tablespoons flour + 2 tablespoons butter thickens 1 cup broth
                         OR
         1/4 cup flour + 1/4 cup butter thickens 1 quart broth

If you're new at this, measure the broth first to determine the amount of flour and butter you'll need.

Three different ways to do this are (making sure to use the formula above):

(1) **Make a paste of equal parts butter and flour**; whisk into simmering broth until desired thickness is reached. Cook and stir for 3-4 minutes.

(2) **Make a roux** by heating butter and adding an equal amount of flour; cook and stir until golden brown. Whisk the broth into the roux to thicken.

(3) **Make a slurry** by adding the amount of flour needed to thicken your broth to ice-cold water in a glass jar; cover the jar and shake vigorously. Whisk slurry into simmering broth; cook and stir 3-4 minutes.

**Toasted flour** deepens the flavor of gravies. Preheat oven to 300 degrees. Spoon all-purpose flour onto a shallow baking pan; roast for about 30 minutes, stirring occasionally. Store in an airtight container, and use as needed. Toasted flour has already been cooked in the oven so gravies require less finishing time.

# Scoops of Confidence

## For Poultry, Meat, and Game

When **pan-frying meat**, listen for the sizzle. If you can't hear it, the heat is too low.

I like to use a mixture of half clarified butter and half canola oil for **browning meats**. This combination has a high smoking point. In other words, the pan can be hotter when you add the meat, resulting in an even browning, not burning. Regular butter has milk solids in it that will burn, so don't go there.

How do you **clarify butter**? Just put solid butter in a small saucepan over very low heat. Melt completely. Skim off the foam that appears on the top; discard. Pour off the clear (clarified) yellow liquid into a dish to save, and discard milk solids left in the pan. You can count on losing only about 1/4 of the volume by the clarification process. Clarified butter is a staple I always have on hand in my kitchen. Stored in an airtight jar and refrigerated, it will solidify but remains usable for a long time.

**Rest** after roasting? Yes. During the roasting process, juices run away from the heat toward the center of the meat. Resting allows these juices to redistribute themselves back into all parts of the meat, resulting in a tender, juicy cut.

When shaping ground **beef patties** for grilling or frying, poke a 1/2-inch hole in the center. All the meat will cook evenly; the hole will all but disappear.

To prevent **marinated meat** from sticking to the grill, pat dry with a paper towel and coat with non-stick vegetable spray. A word of caution, though: Do not use vegetable spray anywhere near the grill; it will ignite.

Try using a tall, cylinder-shaped vase for soaking your **wooden skewers** in water. Remaining upright, the wet skewers are easy to access when assembling kabobs for the grill.

Meat or poultry pieces should be patted dry before adding any kind of **breading**. Coat with flour, dip in egg or milk, then coat with breading. Breading will adhere best if allowed to dry for about 15 minutes before cooking.

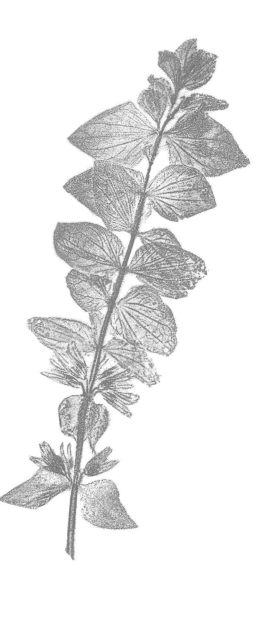

*Origanum marjorana*

(*Marjoram*)

# Vegetables

Green Beans with Feta
Italian Baked Potatoes
Picnic Beans
Oregano Peas
Red Cabbage and Apples
Swiss Potato Bake
Sauerkraut and Brats
Vegetable Fritters

Scoops of Confidence

# Green Beans with Feta

*4 servings*

*Not your Mother's green beans......*

**1 pound fresh green beans, ends removed**
**1 tablespoon canola oil**
**1 tablespoon butter**
**1/2 cup celery, finely diced**
**2 shallots, minced**
**2 cloves fresh garlic, minced**
**1 teaspoon dried basil**
**1/4 teaspoon dried oregano**
**1/4 teaspoon dried marjoram**
**1 1/2 cups fresh tomatoes, chopped**
**2 tablespoons fresh lemon juice**
**1 (4-ounce) package crumbled feta cheese**
**1/2 cup broken cashews (or substitute pine nuts)**

Heat oil and butter in a large skillet. Cook celery for 2 minutes on medium heat. Stir in shallots, garlic, basil, oregano, and marjoram; cook and stir 1 minute. Add green beans; cover, and cook 5-7 minutes or until crisp-tender. Add tomatoes and lemon juice; season with salt and pepper to taste, and simmer additional 2 minutes. Transfer vegetables to a small platter or dish. Sprinkle with feta and cashews.

# Italian Baked Potatoes

*4 servings*

*Variations for this recipe may include toppings of ham, beef, turkey, vegetables, and/or different kinds of cheeses. This is a perfect time to be creative.*

**4 baking potatoes**
**1/2 cup Red Pizza Sauce (or marinara)**
**20 slices pepperoni**
**6 thin slices mozzarella cheese**
**1 cup chopped fresh mushrooms**

Preheat oven to 350 degrees. Scrub potatoes; pierce with a fork in 2-3 places. Bake in oven or microwave (time will vary depending on size your potatoes). Cut a wedge from the top of the hot potato; spoon 1 tablespoon of sauce over the top. Place pepperoni in layers against the inside of potato; sprinkle mushrooms over the pepperoni. Spoon additional tablespoon of sauce over pepperoni or mushrooms. Layer 2 slices of cheese on top. Bake 10 minutes and serve immediately.

# Picnic Beans

*8-10 servings*

*Here is that simple side dish to accompany hot or cold potato salad. My brother Gary claims these as his favorite.*

**1/2 pound bacon (about 8 slices)**
**3/4 cup onion, diced**
**1/4 cup celery, thinly sliced**
**1 (28-ounce) can good quality pork and beans**
**1 (16-ounce) can dark red kidney beans, rinsed and drained**
**1 (16-ounce) can lima beans, rinsed and drained**
**1 (16-ounce) can navy beans, rinsed and drained**
**1/2 cup ketchup**
**1/4 cup good quality bourbon whiskey**
**2 tablespoons Worcestershire sauce**
**1 Tablespoon pure maple syrup**
**1 tablespoon prepared mustard**

Preheat oven to 375 degrees. Cook bacon until crisp; transfer to paper toweling to drain and cool. Reserve about 3 tablespoons of the bacon drippings in skillet. Add onions and celery; cook and stir over medium heat until tender and translucent.

Crumble the cooked bacon. Spoon bacon, onions, celery, pork and beans, kidney beans, lima beans, and navy beans into a 2 1/2-quart casserole. Add ketchup, bourbon, Worcestershire sauce, syrup, and mustard; mix well. Bake, uncovered, in preheated oven for 45 minutes. Serve hot or at room temperature.

# Oregano Peas

*4 servings*

**1 (10-ounce) package frozen green peas**
**4 tablespoons butter**
**1 cup fresh mushrooms, sliced**
**1 tablespoon minced onion**
**1/2 teaspoon kosher salt**
**1/2 teaspoon oregano**
**1/4 teaspoon seasoned salt**
**1/4 teaspoon coarse black pepper**

Cook peas until tender. Melt butter in skillet; add mushrooms, onions, kosher salt, oregano, seasoned salt, and pepper; cook and stir until mushrooms are tender. Stir in cooked peas; serve immediately.

COOKING WITH CONFIDENCE

# Red Cabbage and Apples

*An excellent, do-ahead and reheat side dish.*

6 servings

8 strips lean bacon, cut into 1/2-inch pieces
3/4 cup yellow onion, diced
1/2 cup celery, diced
3 tablespoons brown sugar
2 tablespoons all-purpose flour
1/4 cup red wine vinegar
1/2 cup red wine
4 cups red cabbage, shredded
1 teaspoon salt
1/4 teaspoon freshly ground black pepper
2 cups tart apples (such as Granny Smith), peeled and cubed

Cook bacon until crisp in a large Dutch oven or stockpot. Add onions and celery; cook and stir over medium heat for 3 minutes. Whisk in sugar, flour, vinegar, and red wine; cook additional minute until well blended. Add cabbage, salt, and pepper; mix well. Cover pot with a tight lid; cook 20 minutes, stirring occasionally. Add apples, cover once again; cook additional 10 minutes. Serve hot.

# Swiss Potato Bake

Serves 6

*Delicious with barbequed beef or ribs.*

2 1/2 pounds red potatoes, peeled and sliced thin (do not rinse)
6 tablespoons butter, divided
2 tablespoons fresh parsley, chopped
3/4 teaspoon kosher salt
1/2 teaspoon freshly ground black pepper
1/2 cup green onions, thinly sliced
1 cup (about 4 ounces) shredded Gruyere cheese
1/2 cup grated Parmesan cheese
1 1/4 cups beef broth, boiling

Preheat oven to 425 degrees. Use 2 tablespoons of the butter to coat the inside of a 2-quart casserole. Combine parsley, salt, pepper, onions, and cheeses in a small bowl; set aside.

For the first layer, pat about 1/2 of the potatoes dry with a paper towel; place slices in the casserole. Sprinkle with half of the parsley and cheese mixture. Dot with 2 tablespoons butter. Repeat process with remaining potatoes, cheese mixture, and butter. Pour boiling beef broth over the top. Bake 60 minutes or until potatoes are fork-tender, and top is nicely browned.

# Sauerkraut and Brats

*4 servings*

*Even if you wrinkle your nose when someone says sauerkraut, try this for dinner. The idea of using wine instead of brine comes from the Alsace region of northeastern France where (you guessed it) they make a good amount of Reisling. The restaurants serve sauerkraut family style with sausages, boiled potatoes, and an absolutely huge cut of pork -- in ample, German-style portions. Key ingredients here are the Reisling (California Reislings are wonderful) and the coriander.*

**1 (24-ounce) package sauerkraut***
**6 slices bacon, cut in 1/2-inch dice**
**2 tablespoons butter**
**1/2 cup chopped onions**
**1/2 cup finely chopped celery**
**2 cloves fresh garlic, minced**
**2 cups Reisling wine**
**1 teaspoon dried coriander**
**1 teaspoon granular chicken bouillon**
**1/2 teaspoon freshly ground black pepper**
**5 or 6 precooked bratwurst or kielbasa**

Preheat oven to 350 degrees. Butter a 2 1/2-quart baking dish; set aside.

Cook bacon pieces in a skillet over medium heat until brown and crisp; transfer to a paper towel to drain. Add butter to skillet along with onions and celery; cook and stir for 3 minutes. Add garlic; cook 1 more minute. Rinse sauerkraut with cold water; drain thoroughly. Mix drained sauerkraut with bacon, onions, celery, garlic, and wine. Stir in coriander, chicken bouillon, and pepper.

Place sausages on the bottom of prepared baking dish; spoon the sauerkraut mixture over the top. Cover the baking dish; bake 45 minutes. Remove the cover; bake additional 15 minutes. Serve hot.

\*      Look for the packaged sauerkraut in your supermarket's meat department. For this recipe, don't try to substitute canned sauerkraut.

COOKING WITH CONFIDENCE

# Vegetable Fritters

*8 (3-inch) fritters*

*Try these with barbequed ribs or chicken -- they're pretty, and delightfully easy to make. To save time, use a small food processor to grate the potatoes and carrots.*

**2 eggs**
**1 teaspoon bottled hot sauce**
**1 cup fresh or frozen corn kernels**
**1/4 cup fresh or frozen peas**
**1/4 cup green onions, thinly sliced**
**1 cup raw potatoes, shredded**
**3/4 cup raw carrots, shredded**
**1/4 cup fresh parsley, chopped**
**1/2 teaspoon dried dill weed**
**1/2 cup all-purpose flour**
**1/2 teaspoon kosher salt**
**1/4 teaspoon freshly ground black pepper**
**2 tablespoons butter**
**1 tablespoon vegetable oil**

Beat eggs in a medium mixing bowl; stir in hot sauce. Add corn, peas, onions, potatoes, carrots, parsley, and dill weed; mix well. Stir in flour, salt, and pepper.

Melt 1 tablespoon of the butter and about 1/2 tablespoon oil in a large skillet. Using a 1/4 cup measuring cup, dip out four portions of the fritter mixture and place in the hot skillet; flatten each slightly with a spatula. Cook 3 minutes on the first side over medium heat; turn each fritter, lower heat a bit and cook additional 3 minutes.

Transfer fritters to a warm plate. Turn the heat up to medium once again; add remaining butter and oil. Measure out the other four fritters, flattening and cooking as the first batch.

Serve warm with a small dollop of yogurt or sour cream.

# Scoops of Confidence

## For Vegetables

For crisp, long-lasting **celery**: Cut root end off. Wash and trim each stalk. Wrap in paper towel (the package will be damp, and that's okay). Wrap tightly in foil. Refrigerate. **Rescue limp celery** by placing in ice water + 2 tablespoons granulated sugar for 1 hour. Miracle.

**To roast vegetables,** preheat oven to 425 degrees. Cut all vegetables about the same size. Toss with a little olive oil, salt, and pepper. Spread in single layer on a baking sheet with no (or low) sides. Pop into the oven, stir after 10 minutes; roast additional 10-15 minutes or until fork-tender.

For a quick side dish, mix 1/4 cup butter, 2 tablespoons horseradish, 2 tablespoons whole-grain mustard, 1 teaspoon brown sugar, and 1/4 cup fresh, chopped parsley. Toss with roasted vegetables; serve hot. OR try tossing roasted carrots with brown sugar and orange juice. Yummy.

**Store potatoes and onions** separately, and not in plastic bags. Moisture from the potatoes will spoil the onions; ethylene gas from the onions make the potatoes sprout. Ideal conditions? Potatoes store well in a 40 degree temperature and high humidity, and onions prefer a 35 degree temperature with low humidity.

Refrigerating **tomatoes** compromises their flavor and texture. No sunshine? Ripen green tomatoes by placing them in a paper bag with an apple for 2-3 days at room temperature.

If you're confused as to whether **vegetables** should begin cooking in cold or boiling water, here's an easy, reliable guide: For those vegetables grown underground (potatoes, carrots, onions), use cold water. For vegetables grown above ground (peas, broccoli, beans), use boiling water.

After a clove of **fresh garlic** has been peeled, cut it in half lengthwise. If there is a green shoot (sprout) in the center, remove it. The sprout is bitter, and will adversely affect the taste.

When steaming **cauliflower,** add a tablespoon of lemon juice to the water to keep it white.

COOKING WITH CONFIDENCE

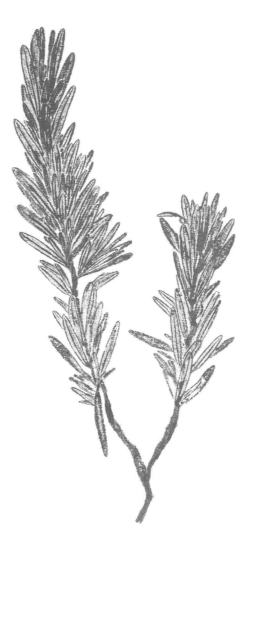

*Rosmarinus officinalis*

(Rosemary)

# Sweets

Brown Sugared Apple Cake
Butterscotch Pecan Cake
Crumble Cake
Flourless Chocolate Cake
Lemon Cream Cheese Cake
Sour Cream Chocolate Cake

Amaretto Cheesecake
Pumpkin Cheesecake
Strawberry Cheesecake

Lemon Berry Pie
Northern Blueberry Pie
Pecan Pie

Bread Pudding
Frozen Chocolate Dessert
Peach Crisp
Quick Apple Dessert
Raspberry Cream Cheese Delight
Rhubarb Meringue Dessert
Cheesecake Squares
Strawberry Meringue Torte

Lemon Bars
Raspberry Almond Squares
Sour Cream Raisin Bars

Coconut Fork Cookies
Crispy Sugars
Double Chocolate Cherry
Frosted Citrus Dreams
Ginger Snaps from the Farm
Pecan Praline Delights

Scoops of Confidence

# Brown Sugared Apple Cake

*My sister Delores calls this her favorite dessert. It has a wonderful texture and delicious taste. Serve this in small portions; there are a few calories in the frosting.*

*Cake:*
1 1/2 cups brown sugar
2/3 cup vegetable oil
2 eggs
1 teaspoon vanilla
1 cup buttermilk
3 cups flour
1 teaspoon baking soda
1 teaspoon cinnamon
1/2 teaspoon nutmeg
1/8 teaspoon cloves
2 1/2 cups apples, peeled and chopped (about 3 medium)

*Filling and Frosting:*
1 (8-ounce) package cold cream cheese
1/2 cup confectioners' sugar
2 cups heavy cream
1 1/2 tablespoon pure maple syrup

*Garnish:*
1 1/2 cups ground walnuts, toasted in 350 degree oven for 7 minutes

Preheat oven to 350 degrees. Grease and flour 2 (8-inch) round cake pans; set aside.

For the cake, mix brown sugar and oil in a large bowl until smooth. Stir in eggs, vanilla, and buttermilk; beat well. In a separate bowl, combine flour, soda, cinnamon, nutmeg, and cloves. Stir the flour mixture into the egg mixture until no visible traces of flour remain. Fold in chopped apples. Spoon half of the batter into each of the prepared pans. Bake 40-45 minutes until the center of the cake springs back when lightly touched. Let rest in pans for 5 minutes, then turn out onto a wire rack to finish cooling. Toast ground walnuts; set aside.

For the filling and frosting, beat cold cream cheese and sugar until smooth. While mixer is running, gradually add cream; beat until stiff peaks form. Stir in cinnamon and maple syrup; blend well. Turn one cake layer top side down on a plate; spread with about 1/4 of the filling. Place the second layer on top; spread top and sides of both layers with remaining frosting. Garnish with toasted nuts; refrigerate several hours before serving.

# Butterscotch Pecan Cake

*A wonderfully firm cake that slices and serves easily. Lovely with a just a little ice cream.*

## Cake:
2 1/2 cups granulated sugar
1 cup vegetable shortening
1/2 cup butter, softened
4 eggs
1 cup low fat buttermilk
1 tablespoon good quality bourbon
3/4 teaspoon baking soda dissolved in 1 tablespoon water
3 1/2 cups all-purpose flour
1 teaspoon cinnamon
1/2 teaspoon kosher salt
1/2 teaspoon nutmeg
1/4 teaspoon cloves
1/4 teaspoon allspice

## Caramel Frosting:
1/2 cup butter
1 cup brown sugar, packed
1/3 cup evaporated milk (or cream)
2 cups confectioners' sugar
1/4 cup pecan halves

Preheat oven to 300 degrees. Generously grease and flour a bundt pan; set aside.

Combine sugar, shortening, and butter in a large bowl; beat until creamy and light. Add eggs, 1 at a time, beating well after each addition. Add buttermilk, bourbon, and dissolved soda; mix well. In a separate bowl, stir flour, cinnamon, salt, nutmeg, cloves, and allspice together. Beat flour mixture into the buttermilk mixture forming a thick, creamy batter. Spoon into prepared pan. Bake 1 hour and 30 minutes or until toothpick inserted in the center of cake comes out clean. Allow to rest in pan for 5 minutes, loosen edges with a knife, and turn out onto a wire rack to cool.

For the frosting, combine butter and brown sugar in a saucepan; heat to boiling. Carefully add milk (mixture will sizzle); cook and stir 2 minutes. Remove from heat, pour frosting into a mixing bowl, and cool to room temperature. Gradually add confectioners' sugar; beat until thick and smooth. Spread frosting on top of cake, drizzling some down the sides. Garnish with pecans.

COOKING WITH CONFIDENCE

# Crumble Cake

*12 servings*

*My brothers Virgil and Leonard consider this to be their favorite food from home on the farm - an eggless cake with a nice, brown sugary taste. I believe the recipe dates back to the 1930s.*

## First mixture:

1 cup brown sugar, packed
1 cup granulated sugar
1/3 cup shortening
1/3 cup butter
1 cup all-purpose flour
1 tablespoon cinnamon

## Second mixture:

1 cup buttermilk
1 teaspoon soda
1 teaspoon pure vanilla extract
1 3/4 cup all-purpose flour

Preheat oven to 350 degrees. Lightly grease a 9 x 13-inch cake pan; set aside.

In a large bowl, combine brown sugar, granulated sugar, shortening, butter, flour and cinnamon; work with fork or pastry blender to form a crumbly mixture. Remove 3/4 cup of the mixture and set aside. To remaining portion, add buttermilk, soda, vanilla and flour; mix well.

Spoon batter into prepared pan; sprinkle reserved crumbs evenly over the batter. Bake 30 minutes or until top springs back when touched lightly in the center.

# Flourless Chocolate Cake

*16-20 servings*

*Just like fudge, this is the ultimate chocolate dessert.*

<u>Cake:</u>
**1 cup granulated sugar**
**3/4 cup butter, softened**
**10 eggs**
**32 (1 ounce) squares semisweet chocolate, chopped**
**2 teaspoons coffee liqueur (or 2 teaspoons pure vanilla extract)**

<u>Glaze:</u>
**1/2 cup + 2 tablespoons heavy cream**
**8 (1 ounce) squares semisweet chocolate, chopped**

<u>Raspberry Sauce:</u>
**2 (10 ounce) packages frozen raspberries in syrup, thawed**

<u>Garnish:</u>
**Fresh raspberries and fresh mint**

Preheat oven to 350 degrees. Grease the bottom of a 10-inch springform pan; line bottom with parchment paper. Wrap bottom of pan with foil to prevent any possible leakage in the oven; set aside.

For the cake, melt chocolate in a heavy saucepan over very low heat; set aside to cool slightly. In a large bowl, blend sugar and butter; beat at medium speed 2 minutes or until light and fluffy. Add eggs, one at a time, beating after each addition until well blended. Add melted chocolate; beat additional minute or until batter is thick and smooth. Stir in liqueur or vanilla.

Pour into prepared pan; bake 60-70 minutes or until knife inserted in the center comes out almost clean. The cake will sink slightly in the center and will have cracks at the edges. This is normal. (Remember, you have no flour in this batter). Cool cake on wire rack for 5 minutes. Gently press down edges of cake and run a sharp knife around top edge to loosen it from the pan. Refrigerate in the pan 6-24 hours to chill and set.

Run a knife all around the edge of the cake; remove side of pan. Invert cake on a flat serving plate. Remove bottom of the pan and peel off parchment paper. For the glaze, heat cream to boiling. Remove from heat; add chopped chocolate and stir until chocolate has melted. Spread glaze onto the cake. (Glaze will set up in 15 minutes). For the sauce, puree raspberries and syrup (one package at a time) in a blender or food processor. Press raspberries through a strainer to remove seeds, and stir well to blend. Cover, and chill.

Bring cake to room temperature. Cut into small wedges using a hot, dry knife. Spoon raspberry sauce onto each serving plate. Transfer cake wedge to each plate; garnish with fresh berries and a sprig of mint.

COOKING WITH CONFIDENCE

# Lemon Cream Cheese Cake

*12 servings*

*This cake is one of my all-time favorites. It has a lovely flavor and, because of the cream cheese and eggs, slices beautifully. I prefer a lemon frosting; however, you may choose to use the alternate glaze recipe.*

## Cake:
1 (8-ounce) package regular cream cheese, softened
1 1/2 cups unsalted butter, softened
2 1/2 cups granulated sugar
1/4 cup fresh lemon juice
1 1/2 tablespoons freshly grated lemon rind
1 1/2 tablespoons pure vanilla extract
1 teaspoon pure lemon extract
6 eggs
3 cups all-purpose flour
1/4 teaspoon kosher salt

## Frosting:
1 (8-ounce) package cream cheese, softened
2 tablespoons butter, softened
2 teaspoons freshly grated lemon rind
2 teaspoons lemonade concentrate, thawed
3 1/2 cups confectioners' sugar

## Garnish:
fresh lemon peel cut in very thin strips

Preheat oven to 350 degrees. Generously grease and flour a bundt pan; set aside.

For the cake, beat cream cheese and butter together in a large bowl until smooth and light. Add sugar; beat 3 minutes until fluffy. Stir in lemon juice, rind, vanilla, and lemon extract; blend well. Add eggs, 2 at a time, beating slightly after each addition. Add flour and salt; beat until just well blended.

Pour into prepared pan. Bake 1 hour, 15 minutes, until cake pulls away from the edges of the pan, and a toothpick inserted in the cake comes out clean. Let rest in pan for 5 minutes; turn out onto a wire rack to finish cooling.

For the frosting, beat cream cheese and butter together until light and fluffy. Add lemon rind and lemonade concentrate; beat well. Stir in confectioners' sugar; beat until smooth and creamy. Spread evenly on cake. Garnish with fresh lemon peel cut in thin strips. **Alternate Glaze**: Mix 2 tablespoons lemon juice, 1/3 cup confectioners' sugar, and 1/4 teaspoon vanilla. Spoon over cake.

# Sour Cream Chocolate Cake

*12 servings*

*This cake was made so often at home we all knew the recipe "by heart". It is a favorite of my youngest brother Don.*

## Cake:
1 1/2 cups granulated sugar
1/2 cup cocoa powder
1 cup sour cream
3 eggs, beaten
1 teaspoon pure vanilla extract
2 cups all-purpose flour
2 teaspoons baking soda
1/4 teaspoon salt
1 cup boiling water

## Frosting:
6 tablespoons butter
6 tablespoons milk
1 1/2 cups granulated sugar
1 cup semisweet chocolate chips

Preheat oven to 350 degrees. Generously grease and flour a 9 x 13-inch cake pan; set aside.

For the cake, combine sugar and cocoa; add sour cream, eggs, and vanilla; beat well. In a separate bowl, stir flour, soda, and salt together. Add the flour mixture to the egg mixture; mix well. Stir in boiling water; mix well. Pour batter into prepared cake pan. Bake 40 minutes or until top of the cake springs back when lightly touched.

For the frosting, combine butter, milk, and sugar in a medium saucepan. Bring mixture to a boil over medium heat; cook for 1 minute. Remove from heat. Add chocolate chips; stir until well blended. Cool slightly; beat until mixture thickens to a spreading consistency. Frost cake, and cut in squares to serve.

COOKING WITH CONFIDENCE

# Amaretto Cheesecake

*12-16 servings*

*If you like Amaretto, you'll love this always-dependable dessert.*

## Crust:
**1 1/4 cups vanilla wafer crumbs**
**1/2 cup almonds, very finely chopped**
**6 tablespoons unsalted butter, softened**
**1/4 teaspoon almond extract**

## Filling:
**3 (8-ounce packages) cream cheese, softened**
**1 cup granulated sugar**
**1/8 teaspoon kosher salt**
**1/2 teaspoon pure vanilla extract**
**1/2 teaspoon almond extract**
**1 cup sour cream**
**3 eggs**
**1/4 cup Amaretto liqueur**

## Garnish:
**1/2 cup sliced, toasted almonds**

Preheat oven to 350 degrees.

Mix vanilla wafer crumbs with the almonds, butter and extract. Press into bottom of a 9-inch springform pan. Bake 7 minutes; cool. Maintaining oven temperature at 350 degrees, toast almonds for garnish by baking in an ungreased pan for about 5 minutes, or until lightly browned. Set aside to cool.

For the filling, beat cream cheese until smooth. Add sugar, salt, and extracts; beat well. Add sour cream; beat additional 4-5 minutes until thick and very smooth. Add eggs, 1 at a time, beating until well mixed. Stir in Amaretto; mix well. Spoon filling over baked, cooled crust. Bake 1 hour and 10 minutes until filling is set. The sides should be a bit raised and just beginning to brown. Remove from oven; cool to room temperature. Loosen sides by running a knife around the edge. Refrigerate in the pan 4 hours or longer.

Invert on flat serving plate. Garnish with toasted almonds, slice and serve.

# Pumpkin Cheesecake

*10-12 servings*

*A nice change from pumpkin pie, this will help serve a crowd. I'll bet you'll love the ginger snap crust too. Make ahead of time so it sets well.*

## Crust:

1 1/2 cups crushed gingersnap cookies
3/4 cup hazelnuts
3 tablespoons brown sugar, packed
1 tablespoon crystallized ginger, finely ground
6 tablespoons butter, melted

## Filling:

3 (8-ounce) packages cream cheese, softened
1 cup brown sugar, packed
1 1/2 cups canned pumpkin (not pie filling)
1/2 cup heavy cream
1/3 cup pure maple syrup
1 tablespoon pure vanilla extract
1 teaspoon kosher salt
1 teaspoon ground cinnamon
1/2 teaspoon ground allspice
4 eggs

## Topping:

1 cup heavy cream
3 tablespoons pure maple syrup
1/2 teaspoon vanilla
1/2 teaspoon ground cinnamon

Preheat oven to 350 degrees. Spread the hazelnuts (single layer) in a shallow pan. Bake, stirring occasionally, about 8 minutes, until lightly toasted. <u>Adjust oven temperature to 325 degrees for the cheesecake</u>. Cool hazelnuts completely and rub the skins off with a paper towel; set aside. Wrap the springform pan bottom with foil to prevent leakage in the oven. For the crust, grind the cookies to a fine crumb consistency in a blender or food processor. Add hazelnuts, brown sugar, and ginger; pulse until ground. Pour into a bowl; add butter, and mix until well combined. Press the mixture into the bottom and 2/3 up the sides of a 9-inch springform pan. Bake for 8 minutes until lightly browned. Cool.

For the filling, beat the cream cheese and brown sugar together until light and fluffy. Add pumpkin; mix well. Stir in cream, syrup, vanilla, salt, cinnamon, and allspice; beat until smooth and creamy. Beat in the eggs, one at a time, until just combined.

Pour the batter into the prepared crust. Bake approximately 1 hour and 45 minutes until top is puffed and center is set. Transfer to a wire rack; cool for 10 minutes. Run a knife around the edges to loosen the cheesecake; let cool completely. Cover and refrigerate overnight. When ready to serve, whip cream with syrup, vanilla, and cinnamon until stiff peaks form. Cut cheesecake and serve with whipped cream.

COOKING WITH CONFIDENCE

# Strawberry Cheesecake

*12-16 servings*

*Easy to make, wonderful taste, impressive to serve.*

## Crust:
2 1/2 cups graham cracker crumbs
1/4 cup granulated sugar
1 teaspoon ground cinnamon
3/4 cup butter, melted

## Filling:
4 eggs
4 1/2 (8-ounce) packages cream cheese, softened
3 tablespoons fresh lemon juice
1 1/2 cups granulated sugar
1/2 teaspoon kosher salt

## Topping:
2 pints medium-sized strawberries, washed and hulled

## Glaze:
12 ounces seedless raspberry jelly
1 tablespoon cornstarch
1/4 cup Grand Marnier liqueur
1 tablespoon water

Preheat oven to 350 degrees. Butter a 10-inch springform pan; set aside.

For the crust, combine crumbs, sugar, cinnamon, and butter in a medium bowl; mix well. Press into bottom and partially up the sides of prepared pan.

For the filling, beat the eggs in a small bowl. In a separate large bowl, beat the cream cheese until light and fluffy. Add lemon juice, sugar, and salt; beat until smooth and light. Stir in beaten eggs, blending well. Pour into prepared crust. Bake 60 minutes. To prevent uneven cooling, run a knife along the inside edge of the pan loosening the sides. IMPORTANT: Cool cheesecake in the pan until room temperature; then refrigerate for at least 3 hours to set. Transfer chilled cheesecake to a flat serving plate.

For the glaze, combine a small amount of the jelly with the cornstarch in a small saucepan; mix well. Add remaining jelly, liqueur, and water. Cook over medium heat about 10 minutes until mixture is thick and clear. Cool to lukewarm, stirring occasionally.

To finish the cheesecake, arrange berries (pointed side up) evenly over the top of the cake. Spoon glaze over the berries, allowing some to drip down the sides of the cake. Refrigerate until glaze is set.

# Lemon Berry Pie

*Extremely easy to make - great blend of flavors.*

## Crust:
1 cup all-purpose flour
1/2 cup butter, softened
2 tablespoons granulated sugar
1/4 teaspoon kosher salt

## Filling:
2 large egg whites
2/3 cup granulated sugar
2 teaspoons grated lemon peel
1/4 cup fresh lemon juice
3-4 drops yellow food coloring (optional)
1 cup heavy cream, whipped

## Blueberry Sauce:
2 tablespoons cornstarch
2/3 cup cold water
2/3 cup granulated sugar
1 teaspoon lemon juice
1/8 teaspoon kosher salt
2 cups fresh blueberries

Preheat oven to 350 degrees.

For the crust, combine flour, butter, sugar, and salt until mixture forms a cookie-like consistency. Pat into the bottom and up the sides of a 10-inch pie plate. Bake 15 minutes. Cool on a wire rack.

For the filling, whip egg whites until soft peaks form; add sugar, and whip until stiff peaks form. Fold in lemon peel, juice, coloring, and whipped cream. Spoon filling into prepared, cooled crust. Refrigerate. Pie can be frozen at this point, but must be thawed before serving.

For the sauce, combine cornstarch and cold water. Transfer the cornstarch mixture to a saucepan. Add sugar, lemon juice, salt, and blueberries. Cook and stir over medium heat until mixture is thick and clear. Transfer to a bowl; cover with plastic wrap, and refrigerate.

To serve, slice pie and serve with sauce on the side.

# Northern Blueberry Pie

6-8 servings

*In the forests of northern Minnesota, we are lucky enough to pick our own blueberries. One can really get a stash if the bears leave you alone. You learn rather quickly what "heads up!" really means.*

## Cookie Crust:
3 ounces cream cheese, softened
1 1/3 cups all-purpose flour
1/2 cup butter

## Filling:
5 tablespoons cornstarch
1 cup granulated sugar
1/2 teaspoon kosher salt
1 1/3 cups cold water
6 cups fresh blueberries -- rinsed well and patted dry with a paper towel
3 tablespoons lemon juice
4 tablespoons butter

## Topping:
2 cups heavy cream
3 tablespoons confectioners' sugar
1 teaspoon pure vanilla extract
1/2 cup fresh blueberries for garnish

Preheat oven to 350 degrees.

With a pastry blender or fork, combine cream cheese, flour and butter in a mixing bowl to make a soft, cookie-like dough. Using your hands, form dough into a large flat disc. Transfer disc to a 10-inch pie plate; press evenly into the bottom and and up the sides. Bake15-20 minutes or until crust has lightly browned. Remove from oven; cool on a wire rack.

For the filling, combine cornstarch, sugar, and salt in a large saucepan; add cold water and mix well. Mash 1 cup of the blueberries; add the mashed blueberries + 1 additional cup of blueberries to the cornstarch mixture. Cook and stir over medium  heat about 5-7 minutes until mixture is very thick and clear. Remove from heat; stir in lemon juice and butter.  Transfer filling to a large glass bowl; cool to room temperature. Stir in remaining berries; mix thoroughly. Spoon filling into cooled crust; refrigerate.

For the topping, whip cream, sugar, and vanilla until stiff peaks form; frost top of pie. Slice into serving pieces; garnish each piece with a few fresh blueberries, and serve cold.

# Pecan Pie

*6 servings*

*You will find the filling for this pie easy to make, with a deep buttery pecan flavor that's hard to beat.*

## Pastry: (this recipe makes 3 single crusts; you will need 1 here)
1 1/2 cups all-purpose flour
1/2 teaspoon kosher salt
1/4 teaspoon granulated sugar
1/2 cup shortening
5 tablespoons ice water

## Filling:
1 1/2 cups pecans, divided
1/4 cup butter
3 eggs
2/3 cup granulated sugar
1 cup light corn syrup
1/2 teaspoon lemon juice
1 teaspoon pure vanilla extract
1/8 teaspoon kosher salt
8 or 9-inch unbaked pastry shell

For the pastry, whisk flour, salt, and sugar together. Cut in shortening with a pastry blender until mixture resembles coarse crumbs. Sprinkle ice water over all parts of the mixture; toss quickly with a fork until most of the particles stick together. Do not over-mix. Gather the pastry and form it into a flat disk. Cover with plastic wrap and refrigerate for at least 30 minutes. Divide dough into 3 equal portions. Roll one out on a lightly floured surface, and place in 9-inch pie plate. Use the remaining dough for 2 additional crusts.

Preheat oven to 425 degrees. Coarsely chop about 1 cup of the pecans, reserving the nicest ones for the top of the pie; set aside. For the filling, heat the butter in a small saucepan until it turns nutty brown in color. (Watch carefully so it doesn't burn). Remove from heat and set aside. In a medium bowl, beat eggs well. Add sugar, corn syrup, lemon juice, vanilla, and salt; beat until blended. Stir in the browned butter and chopped pecans; mix well. Pour into unbaked pie shell; top with remaining pecans. Bake 10 minutes. Adjust oven temperature to 325 degrees; bake for additional 40 minutes.

Cool on a wire rack. Cut into wedges and serve cold with sweetened whipped cream or ice cream.

COOKING with CONFIDENCE

# Bread Pudding

6-8 servings

*Another "comfort food" dessert that we love and remember from home.*

## Pudding:
5 1/2 cups bread cubes, toasted
4 cups milk
3 tablespoons butter, melted
3 eggs
1/8 teaspoon kosher salt
1 cup granulated sugar
1 teaspoon cinnamon
3/4 teaspoon nutmeg
1 teaspoon pure vanilla extract

## Caramel Bourbon Sauce:
1 cup granulated sugar
3 tablespoons water
1/4 cup butter
1/2 cup heavy cream
1/8 teaspoon cinnamon
1/4 cup good quality bourbon

Preheat oven to 350 degrees. Butter a 2-quart baking dish; set aside.

Place bread cubes on a baking sheet; toast in the oven for a few minutes until slightly dried and a little brown. Combine toasted bread cubes with milk and butter in a large bowl; allow to stand for 10 minutes. Beat eggs and salt. Add 1 cup sugar, cinnamon, nutmeg, and vanilla; beat until mixture is lemon-colored and light. Stir egg mixture into the bread mixture. Spoon pudding into the prepared pan. Bake 1 hour, or until knife inserted in the center of the pudding comes out clean. Remove from oven; cool completely.

For sauce, combine sugar and water in a small saucepan. Cook over low heat until it turns dark amber in color. Remove from heat; whisk in butter, cream, and cinnamon. Stir in the bourbon; mix well.

To serve, cut pudding in squares. Top with sauce.

# Frozen Chocolate Dessert

*A quick and easy (yet impressive looking) chocolate treat. Always dependable, always delicious.*

## Crust:
1 1/2 cups chocolate cookie crumbs
6 tablespoons butter, melted
1/4 cup walnuts, finely chopped

## Filling:
8 ounces cream cheese, softened
1/2 cup granulated sugar, divided
1 teaspoon pure vanilla extract
2 eggs, separated (fresh or pasteurized)
6 ounces semi-sweet chocolate, melted
1 cup heavy cream, whipped

## Garnish:
1/2 cup walnuts, finely chopped

Preheat oven to 325 degrees.

For the crust, mix crumbs, butter, and walnuts. Pat mixture into the bottom of an 8-inch springform pan. Bake 10 minutes. Remove from oven; set aside to cool thoroughly.

For the filling, mix softened cream cheese, 1/4 cup sugar, vanilla, and egg yolks; beat well. Add melted chocolate and stir well. Beat cream until stiff peaks form; set aside. In a separate, clean bowl, beat egg whites until soft peaks form; gradually add 1/4 cup sugar and beat until stiff peaks form. Gently fold beaten egg whites into chocolate mixture until no visible trace of egg whites remain. Fold in whipped cream. Spoon mixture over cooled crust, and sprinkle with walnuts. Cover with foil or plastic wrap, and place in the freezer for at least 2 hours. To serve, cut in wedges with a warm, dry knife.

# Peach Crisp

*6 servings*

*Make this when you need a dose of fresh fruit flavor. It's the best.*

## Topping:
1 cup all-purpose flour
3/4 cup regular rolled oats
1/2 cup brown sugar, packed
1/4 cup granulated sugar
1/4 teaspoon cinnamon
1/8 teaspoon nutmeg
1/8 teaspoon kosher salt
1/2 cup butter, room temperature
1/2 cup almond slices, lightly toasted*

## Peach Filling:
6 cups fresh peaches (about 2 pounds), pitted and sliced 3/4-inch
1/3 cup granulated sugar
1 1/2 tablespoons cornstarch
1 tablespoon lemon juice
1/8 teaspoon nutmeg
1/8 teaspoon almond extract

Preheat oven to 375 degrees.

For the topping, stir flour, oats, sugars, cinnamon, nutmeg, and salt together in a large bowl. Add butter. Using a pastry cutter (or fork), mix thoroughly to form coarse crumbs. *To toast almonds, bake 3-4 minutes on an ungreased baking sheet until light brown (watch carefully - they brown quickly). set aside to cool.

For filling, combine peaches and sugar. Mix cornstarch and lemon juice; stir into peaches. Add nutmeg and almond extract; stir well.

To assemble, pour filling into a 9-inch square baking dish. Combine almonds with topping; sprinkle about half of the mixture evenly over the fruit. Pat down lightly. Bake 20 minutes. Remove from the oven; add remaining topping, and bake additional 25-30 minutes or until fruit pierces easily with a toothpick. Allow to set about 30 minutes. Serve warm with ice cream or sweetened whipped cream.

# Quick Apple Dessert

*6 servings*

*This is quick. Wonderful with ice cream.*

## Cake:
1 egg
1/2 cup granulated sugar
1/2 cup all-purpose flour
1/2 teaspoon kosher salt
1 teaspoon baking powder
3/4 teaspoon cinnamon
1 cup chopped apples
1/2 cup chopped walnuts

## Topping:
2 tablespoons brown sugar
2 tablespoons quick cooking rolled oats
2 tablespoons all-purpose flour
2 tablespoons butter

Preheat oven to 350 degrees. Grease a 9-inch glass pie plate; set aside.

For the cake, beat egg and sugar in a medium bowl until creamy. Add flour, salt, baking powder, and cinnamon; mix well. Fold in apples and walnuts. Spoon into prepared dish.

For the topping, combine brown sugar and oats in a small bowl; add flour and butter and mix until crumbly. Sprinkle evenly on batter. Bake 30 minutes or until top springs back when lightly touched.

Cut into wedges and serve hot or cold.

# Raspberry Cream Cheese Delight

*12 servings*

*Wonderful all-around dessert. Tastes equally as good if strawberries are used in place of raspberries.*

## Crust:
1 cup melted butter
1 1/2 cups all-purpose flour
2 tablespoons granulated sugar
1 cup finely crushed pecans

## Raspberry Layer:
1 (3-ounce) package raspberry gelatin
1 cup boiling water
2 (10-ounce) packages frozen raspberries in heavy syrup, thawed

## Cream Cheese Layer:
1 (8-ounce) package cream cheese, softened
1/2 cup butter, melted
2 cups confectioners' sugar

## Top Layer:
2 cups heavy cream
2 tablespoons confectioners' sugar
1 teaspoon pure vanilla extract
1 cup chopped pecans
Fresh raspberries for garnish

Preheat oven to 350 degrees. Mix all crust ingredients together; pat evenly into the bottom of a 9 x 13-inch pan. Bake 20 minutes or until very light brown. Cool thoroughly.

While crust is baking, prepare the raspberry layer: In a medium bowl, mix gelatin in hot water until dissolved. Add raspberries; mix well, and refrigerate one hour until mixture is slightly thickened.

In a small, deep bowl, beat cream cheese, butter, and sugar until light and creamy.

To assemble: Spread the cream cheese mixture over cooled crust. Spoon the thickened raspberry mixture over the cream cheese layer, spreading all the way to the edges and evenly distributing raspberries. Chill until set. Whip cream with sugar and vanilla; spread over raspberry layer. To serve, cut into squares; sprinkle with pecans. A few fresh raspberries on the dessert plate add a lovely accompaniment.

# Rhubarb Meringue Dessert

*8 servings*

*What a delight when you can use rhubarb straight out of the garden. A nice tart/sweet combination.*

## Crust:
1/2 cup butter
1 tablespoon confectioners' sugar
1 cup flour
1/8 teaspoon kosher salt

## Filling:
1 cup granulated sugar
3 tablespoons all-purpose flour
3 egg yolks, beaten
1 tablespoon lemon juice
2 1/2 cups diced fresh rhubarb
1/2 cup half and half
1/8 teaspoon kosher salt

## Meringue:
3 egg whites
1/8 teaspoon cream of tartar
1/8 teaspoon kosher salt
4 tablespoons granulated sugar
1/2 teaspoon pure vanilla extract

Preheat oven to 350 degrees.

For the crust, mix butter, sugar, flour, and salt with a pastry blender or fork. Pat into bottom of a 9-inch square baking pan. Bake 12-15 minutes. Remove from oven. Adjust oven temperature to 375 degrees.

For the filling, mix sugar, flour, beaten egg yolks, lemon juice, rhubarb, cream, and salt in a medium saucepan. Cook over medium heat, stirring occasionally, until thick. Pour cooked filling over baked crust.

For the meringue, beat egg whites with cream of tartar and salt until soft peaks form. Gradually add sugar and vanilla; continue beating until stiff peaks form. Spread meringue over filling. Return dessert to the oven and bake until meringue turns a delicate brown. Cool thoroughly; cut into squares to serve.

COOKING WITH CONFIDENCE

# Cheesecake Squares

*2 dozen squares*

*A very easy-to-prepare, easy-to-serve dessert; perfect for buffets.*

## Crust:
1/2 cup butter, softened
1/4 cup brown sugar, packed
1 cup finely crushed pecans
1 cup all-purpose flour

## Cheesecake Layer I
2 (8 ounce) packages cream cheese, softened
1 cup granulated sugar
3 eggs
1 1/2 teaspoons pure vanilla extract

## Cheesecake Layer II
2 cups sour cream
1/3 cup granulated sugar
1 teaspoon pure vanilla extract

## Garnish:
**Fresh seasonal fruit; peeled, sliced (kiwi, strawberries, raspberries or blue berries)**

Preheat oven to 375 degrees. Coat a 9 x 13-inch pan with non-stick cooking spray; set aside. For crust, combine butter, brown sugar, pecans, and flour in a bowl; mix well. Pat into bottom of prepared pan. Bake 10 to 15 minutes or until light brown.

For Layer I, combine the cream cheese, sugar, eggs, and vanilla; beat until smooth, thick, and creamy. Spread over the baked crust; bake 20 minutes. Cool in the pan on a wire rack for 30 minutes.

For Layer II, combine sour cream, sugar, and vanilla and mix well. Spread over the cream cheese layer. Bake 15 minutes; cool to room temperature on wire rack, then refrigerate for several hours.

To serve, cut into squares using a moistened knife. Garnish each square with fresh fruit of your choice.

# Strawberry Meringue Torte

*A lovely cake, with fresh fruit and cream.*

## Cake:
1/2 cup granulated sugar
1/4 cup butter, softened
4 egg yolks, beaten
1 teaspoon pure vanilla extract
1 cup all-purpose flour
1/4 teaspoon kosher salt
2 teaspoons baking powder
1/4 cup milk

## Meringue:
4 egg whites
1/4 cup granulated sugar
1/4 cup walnuts, toasted and chopped

## Filling:
1 1/2 pints fresh strawberries, sliced
1 tablespoon granulated sugar
1 pint heavy cream
2 tablespoons confectioners' sugar

## Garnish:
1/2 pint fresh, whole strawberries

Preheat oven to 350 degrees, Generously grease and flour 2 (8-inch) round cake pans; set aside.

Combine sugar and butter in bowl; beat until creamy and light. Add egg yolks and vanilla; mix well. In a separate bowl, stir flour, salt, and baking powder together. Add flour mixture alternately with milk to the butter mixture (batter will be very thick). Spread half of the batter into each prepared pan; set aside.

Place walnuts on an ungreased baking sheet, and bake 10 minutes; cool, chop, and set aside. For meringue, beat egg whites and sugar until stiff peaks form. Spread half on each of the layers of cake batter; top with toasted walnuts, and bake for 25 minutes. Cool. Loosen cake edges with a knife, and remove from pans.

For filling, combine strawberries and granulated sugar. Combine cream with confectioners' sugar; whip until stiff peaks form. Stir sweetened strawberries and whipped cream together.

Place plain cake layer, meringue side down, on cake plate. Frost with about 3/4 of the strawberry and cream mixture. Place second layer, meringue side up, on top of strawberries and cream. Top with remaining berries and cream. Chill at least 3 hours, allowing flavors to blend and cake to set. To serve, cut in wedges and garnish with fresh berries.

COOKING with CONFIDENCE

# Lemon Bars

*The sweet and tart of it all...An old standby that everyone loves.*

## Crust:
1 cup butter, softened
1/2 cup confectioners' sugar
2 cups all-purpose flour
1/4 teaspoon kosher salt

## Filling:
4 eggs, beaten
1 1/2 cups granulated sugar
1/3 cup all-purpose flour
1/2 cup lemon juice
2 teaspoons freshly grated lemon zest

1 1/2 tablespoons confectioners' sugar for topping

Preheat oven to 350 degrees.

For the crust, combine butter, sugar, flour, and salt; mix well. Pat into bottom of 13 x 9-inch baking pan. Bake 15 minutes until crust is just beginning to brown. Remove from oven and set aside.

For the filling, beat eggs in a medium mixing bowl until light and lemon colored. Add sugar, flour, lemon juice, and zest; beat until well blended. Pour filling over baked crust; return to the oven and bake additional 20 minutes. Dust the top with confectioners' sugar; transfer to wire rack to cool. Cut in squares to serve.

# Raspberry Almond Squares

*16 servings*

*The flavor combination of raspberry and almond is one you will love. Easy to make, pretty to serve.*

## Crust:
1/4 cup brown sugar, packed
1/2 cup butter, softened
1 cup all-purpose flour
3/4 cup good quality seedless raspberry preserves

## Filling:
2/3 cup granulated sugar
1/2 cup butter, softened
2 eggs
1/2 teaspoon pure almond extract
1/2 cup all-purpose flour

## Frosting:
1/2 cup sliced almonds, toasted*
1/4 cup butter, softened
1 teaspoon pure almond extract
1 1/2 tablespoons milk or cream
1 1/2 cups confectioners' sugar

Preheat oven to 350 degrees.

For the crust, combine brown sugar, butter, and flour; mix well to a cookie dough-like consistency. Press into the bottom of a 9 x 9-inch baking pan. Bake 8 minutes until light brown in color. Remove from oven. While crust is still warm, spoon preserves evenly over the crust, gently spreading to cover.

For the filling, combine sugar, butter, eggs, and almond extract in a medium mixing bowl; beat until smooth and creamy. Add flour; mix well. Spoon and spread filling evenly over layer of preserves. Bake 25 minutes until light golden brown. Loosen edges of bars with a knife while still warm, then cool thoroughly.

For frosting, *toast almonds on an ungreased baking sheet about 5 minutes or until light golden brown; remove from oven and set aside. Mix butter, almond extract, milk, and confectioners' sugar until smooth. Spread evenly on cooled bars; sprinkle with reserved toasted almonds. Cut in squares to serve.

COOKING WITH CONFIDENCE

# Sour Cream Raisin Bars

*16 servings*

*This recipe is a "thumbs up", long-time favorite of my sister Marlys. If you like sour cream raisin pie, you'll love these babies.*

## Crust:
1 cup brown sugar, packed
1 cup butter, softened
1 3/4 cups all-purpose flour
1 teaspoon baking soda
1 3/4 cups quick-cooking rolled oats

## Filling:
2 cups dark raisins
1/4 cup bourbon (or apple juice)
1 cup granulated sugar
1 1/2 tablespoons cornstarch
1 1/2 cups sour cream
3 egg yolks, slightly beaten
1 teaspoon pure vanilla extract

Preheat oven to 350 degrees. Grease a 13 x 9-inch baking pan; set aside.

"Plump" the raisins by combining them with the bourbon in a small saucepan. Bring to a boil over medium heat; immediately reduce heat, and simmer for 10 minutes. Remove pan from heat; set aside. Do not drain.

For the crust, stir brown sugar and butter together in a medium bowl until well mixed. Add flour, soda, and rolled oats; stir well until mixture resembles coarse crumbs. Pat 1/2 of the crumbs firmly into bottom of prepared pan. Bake 7-9 minutes until golden brown. Transfer to a cooling rack.

For the filling, combine sugar and cornstarch in a medium saucepan. Stir in sour cream and beaten egg yolks. Cook and stir over medium heat until mixture is thick and creamy. Add raisins and vanilla; stir to mix well. Spoon evenly over baked crust. Sprinkle remaining oat mixture evenly over the filling; gently pat down to firm. Return pan to the oven; bake additional 30 minutes until golden brown. Transfer to a cooling rack; cool completely before cutting into bars.

# Coconut Fork Cookies

*Makes 4 dozen*

*I remember making these when I was about 9 years old. They still make the cookie jar cover go "clunk" in the middle of the night.*

1 cup brown sugar
1 cup granulated sugar
1 cup shortening
2 eggs, separated
2 cups all-purpose flour
1 teaspoon baking powder
1 teaspoon baking soda
1/2 teaspoon salt
2 cups sweetened coconut
2 cups quick cooking rolled oats

Preheat oven to 350 degrees.

In a large mixing bowl, combine sugars and shortening; beat to a creamy consistency. Separate egg whites from the yolks. Place whites in a narrow, deep bowl; set aside. Add egg yolks to the sugar mixture; beat well. In a separate bowl, combine flour, baking powder, soda, and salt. Add the flour mixture to the sugar mixture, blending well. Stir in coconut and rolled oats - mixture will be very dry and crumbly.

Beat reserved egg whites until stiff peaks form; fold into dough until no trace of egg whites remain.

Roll into balls about 2 inches in diameter. Knead the dough back and forth in your hands if it doesn't want to stick together. Place the dough balls on ungreased baking pans. Using a fork that has been dipped in sugar, crisscross each ball and flatten to about 3/8-inch thick. Bake 15-18 minutes until tops and edges are light golden brown.

Remove from oven; let the cookies remain on the pan for about 5 minutes before transferring them to a wire rack to finish the cooling process. Store in an airtight container, or freeze until needed.

COOKING with CONFIDENCE

# Crispy Sugars

*Makes 3 dozen*

*These cookies are absolutely melt-in-your-mouth perfect.*

1 cup granulated sugar
2/3 cup vegetable shortening
1/3 cup butter, softened
1 egg
1 teaspoon pure vanilla extract
1/2 teaspoon pure almond extract
2 1/4 cups all-purpose flour
1/2 teaspoon kosher salt
1 teaspoon baking soda
1 teaspoon cream of tartar
1/4 cup granulated sugar for coating the cookies

Preheat oven to 350 degrees.

Combine sugar, shortening, and butter; beat until light and fluffy. Add egg, vanilla and almond extracts; beat until well blended. In a separate bowl, combine flour, salt, soda, and cream of tartar. Add the flour mixture to the egg mixture, stirring well to form a stiff dough.

Form dough into 1 1/2-inch balls. Roll in sugar, and place on ungreased baking pan. Flatten sightly. Bake 12-15 minutes until cookie tops are crackled and just beginning to brown. Transfer to a wire rack to cool. Store in an airtight container, or freeze until needed.

# Double Chocolate Cherry Cookies

*Makes about 30*

*A chocolate-lover's dream --- scrumptious served with a glass of ice cold milk.*

## Cookies:
1/2 cup butter
1 cup granulated sugar
1 egg, beaten
1 1/2 teaspoons pure vanilla extract
1 1/2 cups all-purpose flour
1/2 cup cocoa
1/4 teaspoon kosher salt
1/4 teaspoon baking soda
1/4 teaspoon baking powder
2 (10-ounce) bottles maraschino cherries, drained, with some juice reserved

## Frosting:
1 cup semisweet chocolate chips
1/2 cup sweetened condensed milk
1/4 teaspoon kosher salt
1 teaspoon cherry juice

Preheat oven to 350 degrees. Line baking pans with parchment paper; set aside.

Beat butter and sugar until light and creamy. Add egg and vanilla; mix well. In a separate bowl, combine flour, cocoa, salt, soda, and baking powder; stir well to combine. Add the flour mixture to the egg mixture; stir well to create a stiff dough. Shape dough into 1 1/2-inch balls. Press a cherry into the top of each ball.

For the frosting, combine chocolate chips, milk, salt and cherry juice in a small saucepan. Cook and stir over low heat until chips are barely melted and frosting is smooth and glossy. Top each cookie with about 1 1/2 teaspoons of frosting.

Bake 8-10 minutes or until firm. Cookies are easier to remove if they are allowed to cool about 5 minutes on the pan. Transfer to a wire rack to complete the cooling process.

# Frosted Citrus Dreams

*Makes 3 dozen*

*A refreshing, lemon-orange flavor.*

## Cookies:
1/2 cup vegetable shortening
1/2 cup butter, softened
1 cup granulated sugar
1 egg
2 tablespoons frozen orange juice concentrate, thawed
1/4 cup freshly grated orange peel
3 tablespoons freshly grated lemon peel
2 1/4 cups all-purpose flour
1 teaspoon baking soda
1/2 teaspoon kosher salt

## Frosting:
3 tablespoons butter, softened
1 tablespoon freshly grated orange rind
1 tablespoon freshly grated lemon rind
2 cups confectioners' sugar
1 tablespoon frozen orange juice concentrate, thawed
2 teaspoons milk

Preheat oven to 350 degrees.

In a medium mixing bowl, combine shortening, butter, and sugar; beat until creamy. Add egg and orange juice concentrate; beat until smooth. Stir in orange and lemon rind. In a separate bowl, stir flour, soda, and salt together until well combined; add to egg mixture to form a stiff dough. Form dough into 2 1/2-inch balls; flatten slightly. Place on ungreased baking sheet, at least 2 inches apart. Cookies will continue to flatten while baking. Bake 12-15 minutes until golden brown. Remove from oven, and frost while cookies are still warm.

For the frosting, combine butter, grated orange and lemon rind, sugar, orange juice concentrate, and milk; beat until smooth. Spread on warm cookies with a small spatula. Cool completely; store in an airtight container.

# Ginger Snaps From The Farm

*Makes 5 dozen*

*These have a mild, ginger flavor and freeze well. Mom caught me once throwing these little darlings up in the air during a baking afternoon at home. I knew I was in trouble when one stuck to the kitchen ceiling just as she walked in…*

**1 1/2 cups shortening**
**2 cups granulated sugar**
**1/2 cup light molasses**
**2 eggs, beaten**
**4 cups all-purpose flour**
**1/2 teaspoon kosher salt**
**4 teaspoons baking soda**
**2 teaspoons cinnamon**
**2 teaspoons cloves**
**2 teaspoons ginger**

Preheat oven to 350 degrees.

In a large mixing bowl combine shortening and sugar. Add molasses and eggs; beat until light and fluffy. In a separate bowl, combine flour, salt, baking soda, cinnamon, cloves, and ginger. Add flour mixture to the egg mixture to form a stiff dough.

Roll in 1 1/2" balls; dip balls in sugar to coat. Place on ungreased baking sheets. Bake 12-15 minutes until tops are crackled and somewhat firm. Cool on wire rack.

COOKING WITH CONFIDENCE

# Pecan Praline Delights

*This is my very favorite cookie. They are delightful and highly addictive.*

## Cookies:
1 cup butter, softened
1 tablespoon pure vanilla extract
1 cup sifted confectioners' sugar
2 cups all-purpose flour
1 cup very finely ground pecans*

## Filling:
1/4 cup butter, softened
1/2 cup brown sugar, packed
1/4 cup evaporated milk or light cream
1/4 teaspoon pure vanilla extract
1 cup sifted confectioners' sugar

Preheat oven to 350 degrees.

Mix butter and vanilla together in a medium bowl. Add sugar, flour, and pecans; mix well to a stiff dough. Roll dough into balls 1 1/2 inches in diameter; place on ungreased baking pan. Using your thumb (or a melon baller works well, too), make a deep depression in the center of each ball to hold filling.

Bake 18-20 minutes or until just slightly browned. Cool thoroughly.

For the filling, stir butter and brown sugar together in a medium saucepan. Cook and stir constantly over medium heat until mixture boils for 30 seconds. Remove from heat. Carefully add milk (it will sizzle), vanilla, and sugar. Beat until smooth and creamy. Cool to lukewarm; beat once again to a creamy consistency. Using a small spoon (an infant feeding spoon works well), fill the center of each cookie.

*If you cannot locate pecans already ground, make your own in a small food processor. Measure the amount needed AFTER they are ground, because they're really taking the place of more flour in your recipe.

# Scoops of Confidence

## For Sweets

**Separate egg whites** from the yolks by gently emptying the raw egg into your hand. Cradle the yolk, and let the whites slip through your fingers into a small bowl. Should you drop a bit of egg yolk into the whites before **whipping**, use the corner of a paper towel to touch the piece of yolk - the yolk will adhere immediately. Don't even try to whip whites if there is even a trace of yolk. Yolks have fat in them, and it just won't work. Ever.

**Light brown** and **dark brown sugars** are not always interchangeable in a recipe. Dark brown sugar contains more molasses; therefore, it has a stronger flavor. Store both kinds in an airtight container or they'll get harder than a rock.

**Parchment** wisdom: Sprinkle a few drops of water on a baking sheet before adding the paper - it will slide right into place with no curling. To line the bottom of a springform pan, sandwich the parchment between the rim and bottom and lock into place. No need to cut the paper to size - just tear off the excess.

Sometimes even the most expensive **springform pans** are not leakproof. Use foil to form a guard under your springform pan when making **cheesecakes**. Cut a piece of foil about 4 inches larger than your pan, set the pan on top, and bend the foil up the sides. Goodbye to the messy oven.

For an extra clean cut through **meringue**, score it lightly with a hot, wet knife to melt through the very top, then cut as usual.

Save time when making a variety of cookies: Form dough; **freeze** on parchment-lined baking sheets. Transfer the separately frozen, **unbaked cookies** to a plastic freezer bag. Label should include information as the kind, date made, oven temperature and time required for baking. No need to thaw before going into the oven; just add a few minutes to the baking time.

I prefer using kosher salt in all my cooking and baking. It dissolves faster, and isn't quite as salty tasting. If you wish to use regular table salt with these recipes, use less than the kosher salt amounts recommended.

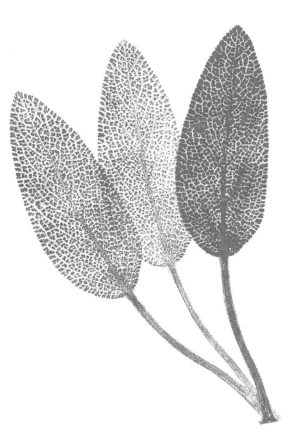

*Salvia officinalis*

*(Sage)*

# Common Weights and Measures

¼ cup  =  **4 tablespoons**  =  2 fluid ounces

1/3 cup  =  **5 tablespoons + 1 teaspoon**  =  2 ½ fluid ounces

½ cup  =  **8 tablespoons**  =  4 fluid ounces

2/3 cup  =  **10 tablespoons + 2 teaspoons**  =  5 fluid ounces

¾ cup  =  **12 tablespoons**  =  8 fluid ounces

1 cup  =  **16 tablespoons**  =  8 fluid ounces

1 pint  =  **2 cups**  =  16 fluid ounces

1 quart  =  **4 cups**  =  32 fluid ounces

COOKING WITH CONFIDENCE

# *Roasting Chart*

### BEEF

Internal Temperature Rare 120, Medium Rare 130, Medium 140
All cuts: Rest, loosely covered with foil, for 20 minutes before carving
Tenderloin: Roasting Temperature 450 degrees
Top loin, Strip Roast, Rib Roast: Roasting Temperature 350 degrees

### PORK

Internal Temperature 155 Medium Well
Tenderloin: Roasting Temperature 400 degrees, Resting Time 5 minutes
Boneless loin: Roasting Temperature 350 degrees, Resting Time 20 minutes

### POULTRY

Internal Temperature 180 degrees
Roasting Temperature 350 degrees

# Emergency Substitutions

| Ingredient | Substitution |
| --- | --- |
| 1 teaspoon baking powder | ¼ teaspoon baking soda + 5/8 teaspoon cream of tartar |
| 1 cup buttermilk | 1 tablespoon lemon juice + enough milk to equal 1 cup Let stand 5 minutes before using. |
| 1 ounce unsweetened chocolate | 3 tablespoons unsweetened cocoa powder + 1 tablespoon melted butter |
| 1 ounce semisweet chocolate | ½ ounce unsweetened chocolate + 1 tablespoon granulated sugar |
| 6 ounces melted semisweet chocolate | ½ cup + 1 tablespoon cocoa powder + ¼ cup + 3 tablespoons granulated sugar + 3 tablespoons butter |
| 1 cup heavy cream | 1/3 cup melted butter + ¾ cup milk |
| 1 cup sour cream | 1 tablespoon lemon juice + enough evaporated whole milk to equal 1 cup |
| 1 tablespoon espresso coffee powder | 1 ½ tablespoon instant coffee powder. The flavor won't be as intense, but will serve the purpose. |
| 1 small clove garlic | 1/8 teaspoon garlic powder |
| 1 ½ teaspoons fresh herbs | ½ teaspoon dried herbs. Exception? Rosemary. Use equal amounts of fresh to dry. |
| 1 cup ketchup | 1 cup tomato sauce + 2 tablespoons granulated sugar + 1 tablespoon vinegar |
| 1 teaspoon prepared mustard | ¼ teaspoon dried mustard + ¾ teaspoon vinegar |
| 1 teaspoon dry mustard | 1 tablespoon prepared mustard |
| 1 cup confectioners' sugar | 1 cup granulated sugar + 1 tablespoon cornstarch, pulsed a few seconds in a blender or food processor |
| 1 cup light brown sugar | 1 cup granulated sugar + 2 tablespoons molasses |
| 1 cup dark brown sugar | 1 cup granulated sugar + 3 tablespoons molasses |
| 1 cup tomato sauce | ½ cup tomato paste + ½ cup water |

COOKING WITH CONFIDENCE

# *Index*

# Index

COOKING with CONFIDENCE

# *Index*

# Index

COOKING with CONFIDENCE

# *Index*

# About the Author

Eunice Naomi Wiebolt was born and raised in Minnesota. Although immersed in the world of business until a few years ago, she has always maintained a passionate interest in cooking, entertaining, recipe research and development. Her culinary background includes training at the Ecole De Gastronomie Francaise, Ritz-Escoffier, in Paris and the Santa Fe School of Cooking, among others.

Her earlier careers included ownership and management of an art and craft retail shop and a full service floral shop. She is a floral design school graduate and Master Florist.

Eunice attended college as a non-traditional student. She holds an Associate in Arts degree with honors from Central Lakes College in Brainerd, Minnesota, and a Bachelor of Science degree in Vocational Education and Business from Bemidji State University in Bemidji, Minnesota.

Over the years she has taught many cooking, business, career, and art classes in both private business and college settings. She currently teaches seasonal seminars on cooking, interior design, and entertaining.

She remains active in the community as a member of a women's service club, a women's investment group, and a book club. She is also a member of the Minnesota Association of Family and Consumer Sciences, Twin Cities Home Economists in Business, Midwest Independent Publishers Association, Small Publishers Association of North America, Publishers Marketing Association, and the Nature Printing Society.

Eunice and her husband Ken enjoy their blended family of five sons, four daughters-in-law, and nine grandchildren. They reside in the Brainerd lakes area of northern Minnesota.

COOKING WITH CONFIDENCE

# COOKING WITH CONFIDENCE

<u>Cookbook Order Form</u>

Your Name   _____

Street   _____

City, State, Zip   _____

Ship To   _____

Street   _____

City, State, Zip   _____

### <u>METHOD OF PAYMENT</u>

_____    Check   (Payable to Romarin Publishing Co.)

_____    Credit Card: Master Card _____    Visa _____

Name as it appears on the card   _____

Card number   _____   Exp. Date _____

Signature   _____

|  | Quantity | Amount Due |
|---|---|---|
| **COOKING with CONFIDENCE** @ $26.95 each | _____ | $_____ |
| Canada @ $42.00 each | _____ | $_____ |
| MN residents add 6.5% sales tax ($1.75 per book) | | $_____ |
| Shipping and Handling (add $5.00 per book) | | $_____ |
| Gift Wrap (add $3.00 per book) | | $_____ |
| Total | | $_____ |

For volume purchases, call (218) 828-0955

Please complete this form and return to:
Romarin Publishing Co.
1945 Red Oak Drive SW
Brainerd, MN 56401-2050

Email: romarin@scicable.com
Website: www.cookingconfidence.com